ADAMS

THE NEW
A-Z OF
MANAGING
PEOPLE

Business titles from Adams Media Corporation

Accounting for the New Business, by Christopher R. Malburg

Adams Businesses You Can Start Almanac

Adams Streetwise Complete Business Plan, by Bob Adams

Adams Streetwise Consulting, by David Kintler

Adams Streetwise Customer-Focused Selling, by Nancy Stephens

Adams Streetwise Do-It-Yourself Advertising, by Sarah White and John Woods

Adams Streetwise Hiring Top Performers, by Bob Adams and Peter Veruki

Adams Streetwise Managing People, by Bob Adams, et al.

Adams Streetwise Small Business Start-Up, by Bob Adams

All-in-One Business Planner, by Christopher R. Malburg

Buying Your Own Business, by Russell Robb

Entrepreneurial Growth Strategies, by Lawrence W. Tuller

Exporting, Importing, and Beyond, by Lawrence W. Tuller

How to Become Successfully Self-Employed, by Brian R. Smith

How to Start and Operate a Successful Home Business, by David E. Rye

Independent Consultant's Q&A Book, by Lawrence W. Tuller

Management Basics, by John & Shirley Payne

Managing People, by Darien McWhirter

Marketing Magic, by Don Debelak

New A-Z of Managing People, by David Freemantle

The Personnel Policy Handbook for Growing Companies, by Darien McWhirter

Presentations, by Daria Price Bowman

Selling 101: A Course for Business Owners and Non-Sales People,
by Michael T. McGaulley

Service, Service, Service: A Secret Weapon for Your Growing Business,
by Steve Albrecht

The Small Business Legal Kit, by J. W. Dicks

The Small Business Valuation Book, by Lawrence W. Tuller

Streetwise Business Forms, by Bob Adams

Streetwise Business Letters, by John Woods

Streetwise Motivating and Rewarding Employees, by Alexander Hiam

Streetwise Time Management, by Marshall J. Cook

Available through your favorite bookseller.

THE NEW
A-Z OF
MANAGING
PEOPLE

David Freemantle

Adams Media Corporation
Holbrook, Massachusetts

Published by
Adams Media Corporation
260 Center Street, Holbrook, MA 02343

ISBN: 1-58062-075-2

Printed in the United States of America.

J   I   H   G   F   E   D   C   B

Library of Congress Cataloging-in-Publication Data
Freemantle, David.
The new A-Z of managing people / by David Freemantle.
p.   cm
ISBN 1-58062-075-2
1. Supervision of employees. 2. Management. I. Title.
HF5549.12.F738 1999
658.3'02 — dc21   98-40305
CIP

This publication is designed to provide accurate and authoritative information
with regard to the subject matter covered. It is sold with the understanding that
the publisher is not engaged in rendering legal, accounting, or other professional
advice. If legal advice or other expert assistance is required, the services of a
competent professional person should be sought.
— From a *Declaration of Principles* jointly adopted by a Committee of the
American Bar Association and a Committee of Publishers and Associations

This book is available at quantity discounts for bulk purchases.
For information, call 1-800-872-5627 (in Massachusetts, 781-767-8100).

Visit our home page at http://www.adamsmedia.com

A Note of Thanks

To Tom and Kate, for their future success
To Pauline, for all my unoriginal sin
To Nora and Harold, my parents, for their invaluable support
And to Mechi and Linnet, for the understanding and hope

Contents

Introduction

You too can be a Superboss. Once you've dipped into this book you'll probably realize you're almost one already.

A lot of people have made a lot of money over the last thirty years or so developing and expounding the idea that to be an effective manager you need to pass psychometric tests, go through assessment centers, attend high-level management training courses and business schools, and, what is worse, even read books on management!

Furthermore over the same period a myth has been perpetrated by the so-called personnel professionals that the only way to manage people is to leave it to them and the unions. The combined efforts of personnel specialists and unions have frequently created a buffer between the boss and his or her people.

But the Superboss doesn't let this stand in the way of managing people successfully. He doesn't hide behind excuses such as the lack of clear personnel policy. You will never hear the Superboss saying, for example, "How can I do a good management job? This company has no career development policy, it doesn't invest in training, and employee relations issues are always dealt with up in Personnel."

The Superboss knows what he has to achieve and sets out to achieve it, overcoming any obstacles put in his way. The Superboss knows how to get his people to support him, irrespective of whether the Chief Executive is crazy, the Vice-President of Finance incompetent, or his immediate boss plain ignorant.

The Superboss doesn't spend his time looking for excuses. He puts up with all the inadequacies of his highly imperfect company and buckles down and does a good job, taking his people with him.

The Superboss has learned a great deal about people. For starters he knows that his own boss is far from perfect and therefore needs a lot of help. He has learned about how people behave, what they respect, what they want. He hasn't learned this by going to school, but by continually questioning his own experience, learning from his own mistakes.

The Superboss has learned that the main determinant in motivating his people is his own relationship with them. As a result he invests a substantial proportion of his time in genuinely developing these relationships. He knows that his staff will judge him by every word he says, every memo he writes, every action he takes, and every decision he makes.

He knows that he needs to be totally consistent in his approach. In fact he knows that it is his behavior, his attitudes, his decisions which will make or break his team — not the behavior, attitudes and decisions of senior executives above, nor the behavior, attitudes and decisions of union officials or those of the Personnel or Finance Departments.

The Superboss knows that the prime factor in his team's motivation and performance is himself, the boss. He will achieve in any circumstances. Over a period of time, the Superboss has developed an extensive range of successful management practices which he knows will lead to maximum team motivation and performance. These do not derive from employee relation strategies, personnel policies, or directives handed down from above. They are actually to do with what a Superboss does minute by minute, hour by hour, to maintain and develop motivation and performance of his total team.

More often than not these management practices are straight forward common sense, a fact often obscured by writers and lecturers on management.

This book attempts to set out an "A to Z" of essential practice for managing people successfully, an "A to Z" of what a manager should actually do to become a Superboss.

The Superboss can just as well be the Chief Executive of an airline as the supervisor in charge of the switchboard or

Production Manager in Factory 2. The Superboss can be responsible for supervising, managing, or directing people whether they number 10, 100, or 10,000.

And of course the Superboss can be male or female. In the text, for simplicity's sake, I have used "he" and "him" to stand for "he or she" and "him or her."

This book is intended not to be read from cover to cover, but "dipped into," perhaps on a page-a-day basis. It is meant to provide, for anyone concerned with managerial excellence, a guide to the action you as a manager can take today toward achieving this and becoming a Superboss.

Once you've dipped into the book a number of times it will be clear that underlying all the entries is a consistent philosophy as to what constitutes successful people management.

As an aspiring Superboss you don't need to wait for the company to enroll you in the next management training course. Start today by putting into practice what you read in this book.

It won't be long before you're a Superboss!

ACCOUNTABILITY

ACCOUNTABILITY IS KNOWING WHAT YOU'LL GET FIRED FOR.

The Superboss goes out of his way to make sure he is 100 percent clear about his accountabilities. He knows what decisions he can make, he knows how to delegate accountability and get members of his team to make decisions.

Whoever makes a decision carries the buck — must be held accountable after the event. Which is why, in poorly-run companies, people try to pass the buck and why inefficient decision-stifling bureaucracies build up. In such companies issues requiring decisions eddy around in a swirling sea of bureaucracy, committees, and upward delegation. The issue will eventually surface with some high-up person who will be forced to say yes or no. That person will then be criticized furiously behind his or her back for making the wrong decision, the critics being the very same people who passed the buck up in the first place.

The Superboss has nothing of this. He'll make a decision and follow through. If he's unclear whether it's his decision or not he'll either check with his boss or preferably make the decision himself. The Superboss has learned that the best way of clarifying gray accountability areas is to make decisions and wait until someone challenges him. That's his opportunity formally to clarify the accountability.

Of course, the Superboss knows that if he makes more than one bad decision he might get fired. Being accountable takes guts!

ACTION TODAY

Sit down today and clarify your own levels of accountability. Make sure you know what business decisions you can make. Better still, make a list of those unresolved issues and start making some decisions; you can account to your boss later. Discuss accountability with your team. Take them out for a drink after work and charge it to the company. See who challenges your decision and then account for that decision.

If you're dissatisfied that you can't authorize travel, recruitment, training, and basic expenditure, go and discuss it with your boss and ensure you are fully clear about your accountabilities when you leave the meeting.

Confirm today that the company is holding you accountable for production levels, sales targets, engineering performance, distribution deadlines, cost-effective administration, or whatever is your line of management.

You need to know today that you are being held accountable for the success of your department, or the failure. If you don't know the difference between success and failure in your area you should resign immediately—either you have an impossible job, or you are an impossible buck-passer.

It starts with you; find out! To be able to manage you must be accountable.

REMEMBER

You are a SUPERBOSS if you can make decision and account for them.

ACHIEVEMENT ACHIEVEMENT IS WHAT MANAGEMENT IS ALL ABOUT.

It's horrifying to interview so many managers who are unable to summarize what they've achieved in their career to date. Some talk about promotion as an achievement. Yes, for them personally. But, I ask, what have they achieved for the company? Then many get lost. Some talk about their skills, or their hard work, what they actually do, week by week.

Achievement is the bench-mark for the Superboss. It is what he has personally contributed, apart from every other manager, to the profitability and success of the company. It's his record and he's proud of it.

His achievements, which he'll measure either quantitatively or qualitatively, might include the successful introduction of a product, or efficiency improvements in the loading bay, or a percentage reduction in labor turnover, or recruiting into the company some of the country's top graduates, or consistent on-time delivery for twelve months, or a reduction in the number of customer complaints from his predecessor's level, or saving the company considerable expenditure by improving the administration.

The Superboss knows that he must achieve to be of any value to the organization. Even routine management functions present achievement opportunities for the Superboss; he will raise standards of housekeeping and output quality (whether that output be a car component or a response to a customer request.)

ACTION TODAY

Draft out your career resume including a summary of your greatest achievements over recent years. If you are unable to identify recent achievements you should be leaving the company before a Superboss catches up with you.

REMEMBER

Achievement differentiates the SUPERBOSS from the "manager ordinaire."

ACTION — ACTION IS THE LANGUAGE OF COMMITMENT; IT SPEAKS LOUDER THAN WORDS.

We've all experienced it. The situation where someone says something will be done and it isn't. The sales manager who promises to call you but doesn't, the service manager who promises to look into your gearbox problem but doesn't, the employee relations specialist who promises to send you a copy of the standard contract of employment, but doesn't.

There's the manager who is always telling you it's someone else's problem. "I can't sort out the scheduling," the manager will tell you, "you'd better see planning."

The Superboss will take action; he'll speak to planning on your behalf. If the Superboss says he'll arrange for a copy of the employment contract to be sent to you, he'll take action; it will be sent to you. If the Superboss promises to send someone to look into your gearbox problem, he'll take action and send someone.

When the Superboss decides to help you he's committed himself to take action. When you take a problem to him ask and for help he assumes that's what you want. He won't refer you to another manager. He won't shrug his shoulders and say, "What can I do?" He won't forget two minutes later what he said. He'll do something about your problem. He'll make a note of the agreed action, and then he'll do what he said he'd do.

If there's a problem his team is struggling with, he'll take action to help. He'll step in and call the chief executive of a company when his team is struggling to obtain supplies from them. He'll see the financial director when the purchasing manager receives continual complaints from a company about excessive delays in payments.

When Lucy Wight asks for five minutes to complain that Public Affairs seems to be blocking her transfer, the Superboss will take immediate action and ring Public Affairs to find out why.

When his boss comes in and mentions that at a dinner last night the president of one of their major customers made some confused comment about service delays, the Superboss will take action. He'll examine the problem and have a report on his boss's desk before the day is out.

The Superboss will always take action.

ACTION TODAY

Take some positive action on every single problem that comes your way. Don't leave it until tomorrow, don't pass it up to your boss, don't leave it for one of your colleagues.

Take action and get the problem fixed, whatever it is. If you see the problem, it's your problem. So take action.

REMEMBER

You will always see a SUPERBOSS where the action is.

ADVICE

HOW CAN A MANAGER FUNCTION WITHOUT ADVICE?

It's not easy to give advice, let alone take it. Certain managers I've met become defensive whenever you offer it. It's as if the process of accepting advice is a process of admitting your own ignorance, exposing your own inadequacies.

Other more assertive managers develop "barriers against advice." They assume an arrogant facade of a thousand answers, appearing to know everything. They will shake their head, frown, and cut you short if you so much as dare to offer advice.

The managers who resist advice normally get their comeuppance when there's an organization change, or a new boss comes in.

The Superboss will give advice, and he'll take it. If he's not in a position to give it, he'll advise where to go for it. His advice is always aimed at helping a person, whether it be to resolve a problem, or improve performance, or whatever. In rendering advice his motives are always honorable, never Machiavellian nor political.

His advice is not always solicited. You might see the Superboss take Ben Giovanni by the elbow to give some gentle advice about not "mouthing off" in front of others. Or when Neil Bloch comes up for a signature he might say, "Sit down, Neil, there's some advice I want to give you. . . ."

On the other hand the Superboss is always taking advice, from his team, from his boss, from his colleagues. If the decision he should make is not perfectly clear he'll seek advice. "Now Neil, perhaps you'll give me some advice. If you were in my shoes what would you do about this problem with allowances . . . ?"

ACTION TODAY

Take advice. Spend your whole day seeking advice from people around you about your three biggest problems. Listen carefully and don't shoot them down if they make crazy suggestions. You don't have to accept their advice, but try very hard to. After all, one or two of them might be in your shoes tomorrow, and even doing a better job than you.

REMEMBER

If you want to be a SUPERBOSS, take advice from one.

AIMS WITHOUT AIMS A MANAGER WILL MISS OUT ON EVERYTHING.

The blind leading the blind. I've seen them stumbling along those long dark corridors of bureaucratic organizations, managers searching for decisions, managers acting as messenger boys between supervisors who need a decision and senior executives who make them.

These managers will tell you one day that revitalizing communications is the highest priority and the next day that it's performance appraisal. They change their priorities constantly. They thoroughly confuse their staff who end up working aimlessly in a contradictory bureaucracy.

The Superboss selects his aim and maintains it. When the Superboss says, "Supervisory training has become our highest priority," you'll still hear him saying it in three or six months time. Everyone will be clear about his aim.

The Superboss does not have all his people rushing blindly in different directions. He connects his aim to the overall profit and people objectives of the business; he ensures it's clear and focused and then communicates it to his people, following through to ensure everyone is moving in the same direction.

If the aim is a notable improvement to customer service, he'll clarify exactly what is required; he'll ensure that all his people are aware of it and push cohesively for that improvement. In six months time when customer service has dramatically improved he might well change his aim, but until then that aim will be maintained and reinforced.

ACTION TODAY

What are your main aims over the next six months? Write them down. You should have no more than six of them. Three would be better.

ACTION TOMORROW

Check with your team that they are 100 percent clear about these aims.

ACTION NEXT WEEK

Take a stroll to the furthest corner of your organization (even if it means stepping into an airplane), and just check that the first person you meet there is clear about your aims, is pointing in the same direction and working towards that end. You might be surprised at the result.

ACTION NEXT MONTH

Maintain these aims and reinforce them.

QUESTION

Is your aim to become a SUPERBOSS? If yes, focus the aim and maintain it.

APPRAISAL

APPRAISAL IS AN INTEGRAL PART OF MANAGEMENT, NOT A SYSTEM EXTERNAL TO IT.

Whoever invented the appraisal form should be jailed. (No wonder he or she remains anonymous.)

Appraisal forms have kept whole personnel empires going for many decades and created a pseudo-science of performance ratings and analysis. Life wouldn't be the same for many personnel people if they couldn't wave a blank appraisal form in the face of a busy manager.

This is no excuse for not appraising people. Appraisal is absolutely essential but you don't really need a bit of paper to do it. If it helps, fine — use two sheets of lined $8^1/2$" x 11".

To the Superboss appraisal is second nature. He does it informally on a daily basis as an integral part of his task of managing people. Once or twice a year he'll appraise his team members more formally by sitting down with each of them and reviewing what they've achieved. He'll encourage them to appraise themselves against the objectives and standards formerly agreed. Furthermore they'll discuss areas for improvement. God help anyone who can't improve!

The Superboss knows that if you require a certain performance level and contribution from an individual, then you must give that individual feedback on whether or not it's being achieved. That's appraisal, that's management.

The Superboss will create a climate of trust and mutual help whereby individuals will readily appraise themselves and discuss methods of improvement.

The Superboss will explain that any questions relating to merit-based pay increases or promotion are a completely separate issue. He knows that if pay is directly linked to appraisal an individual will naturally become defensive, will want to cover up weaknesses (which the Superboss could well help with), and will want to exaggerate strengths.

Therefore, the last thing the Superboss will want is an appraisal system in which he has to rate each manager out of 10. Performance rating in this manner tends to be subjective, de-motivational and, to be honest, pseudo-scientific and irrelevant. Appraisal should be a positive, constructive method of helping an individual do better.

ACTION TODAY

Check your appointment book and make sure you have appraisals scheduled for each member of your team over the next twelve months. If you haven't appraised a member of your team within the last twelve months arrange to do so immediately. Keep a record of the appraisal if you think that helps, but remember, appraisals are not witch hunts, nor insurance records, nor pay determinants.

REMEMBER

The SUPERBOSS doesn't wait for his boss to appraise him, he appraises himself.

ASSESSMENT — YOU CAN ASSESS A MANAGER BY ASSESSING HIS OR HER PEOPLE.

Assessment is relating the person to the job. It is a process of becoming 100 percent clear about what the job entails, specifying the type of person best suited to that job, and making a careful and objective judgment about the person under consideration.

The Superboss devotes considerable time to assessing people, not only for a job, but in the job. The Superboss knows that if he gets the assessment process wrong he cannot succeed. To rush assessment and devote insufficient time to it is to put at peril your company and its people.

The Superboss's assessment is always objective. If a job becomes vacant he'll first assess whether or not the job is really needed. Sometimes he'll surprise himself and find the job can be abolished — other people can cover the task involved. Having confirmed the job, he'll assess very carefully what it entails in terms of duties and responsibilities. He'll also assess the skills, attributes, and experience requirements for the ideal candidate. Finally he'll carefully interview the candidates, obtaining as much information about them as possible in relation to their own skills, attributes, and experience. Where appropriate the Superboss will use tests to help him.

He will always involve other people in the assessment process, knowing that they will see a candidate in a different light than he does. However the final decision will always be his, because only he will be accountable for managing the successful candidate's performance. Once the candidate is in the job the Superboss will assess the new recruit's performance on a continuous basis, helping that person live up to the expectations demonstrated during the initial selection process.

The assessment process is critical for the Superboss. He knows that the best results can only be achieved by a rigorously systematic and objective approach to it. His whole team is a reflection of his assessment capability.

ACTION TODAY

Critically review the way you assess people, not only recruitment or promotion candidates, but also your existing people. Do you really devote enough time to this critical task? Do you always co-operate with Personnel when they try to help you specify what is required? Do you opt out and leave the task to Personnel? Identify at least two ways in which you can improve your approach to assessment. It will be reflected in your results.

QUESTION

Who assesses a person to be SUPERBOSS?

AUTHORITY THE BIG "I AM." THE BIG AUTHORITY. BEWARE!

Authority confers power, and power corrupts. Egos are stretched by authority and inadequate managers seek more of it. They want the authority to spend more, to recruit more, to travel more. They want the authority to do whatever they like. And there's no such authority; there never will be unless you're self-employed.

The exercise of authority is a matter of trust. In organizations rife with distrust authority problems loom very large. People fight for authority, moan and groan about the lack of it. In such organizations managers believe that additional authority will give them additional credibility, will raise their status in the eyes of others, will give them power over people. In such organizations the pursuit and acquisition of authority is a selfish endeavor aimed at personal satisfaction, rather than the best interests of the company and its people.

The Superboss exercises his authority with care and discretion. He seeks only sufficient authority to enable him effectively to discharge his responsibilities and contribute what is required of him by the company. The Superboss doesn't see his authority as "power over his people" but more as a power to make decisions directed towards the goals of the organization. If he feels he has insufficient authority to do his job properly, then he'll try to persuade his boss to delegate more.

Sometimes his boss is not around and the Superboss will take the authority onto his own shoulders, explaining later: "I just had to authorize that trip to Australia; the guy had to depart Friday and you weren't back in the office till Monday."

You will never find a Superboss abusing his authority; in fact his discreet and proper use of it gives him authority in the eyes of his people. They know what authority he has, they don't see him juggling with it, pretending he's got it when he hasn't. Nor do they find he's constantly referring back to his boss: "Well, I'm going to have to ask Bob Hines for his approval."

ACTION TODAY

Clean up your authority levels. Have a chat with your boss about it first, mentioning any areas where you'd find it helpful to have more authority. Then look at the authority you delegate to your people. If you know you need more authority to do your job properly, you can assume the same applies to them. So practice what you preach. If you want more authority from your boss, you must push more down to your people. Do it today, mean what you say.

REMEMBER

The SUPERBOSS is never lacking authority.

AWARENESS   YOU CAN'T SOLVE PROBLEMS UNLESS YOU ARE AWARE OF THEM. MANY MANAGERS ARE SO UNAWARE OF PROBLEMS THEY GET BLOWN UP BY THEM.

It's called the ivory tower syndrome. In some organizations they might refer to the "seventh floor" or "Head Office" in the same way.

It's managers who divorce themselves from reality by spending 80 percent of their time in their offices, reading memos and reports, making telephone calls, receiving them, and attending countless meetings. Somewhere outside is a real world, but they are not aware of it. A real world in their own company. Real people who have real problems. That reality cannot be brought to life by reading reports or attending meetings.

The Superboss is fully aware of events around him. To become aware he doesn't rely on the communications that arrive in his office, nor on the people who knock at his door. The Superboss goes out and about, sees and hears for himself. Problems take on a different perspective that way. When people tell him they're having difficulty with a new filtration system the Superboss goes over and sees for himself. He gets a new perspective — they weren't just moaning as usual about new equipment, but do seem to have a genuine and repetitive flow restriction problem.

By being fully aware the Superboss is in the best position to help and lend support.

But it's not only awareness of physical problems, it's awareness of the employee relations climate, too. The Superboss is aware of his people's feelings, of their concerns and grievances. He moves around, chats to them, listens, becomes aware of what they're thinking. This helps him nip problems in the bud, helps him address issues before they grow into something bigger.

ACTION TODAY

Carry out a team awareness test. Gather your immediate team together, and using a whiteboard or flip-chart ask each person to state what they believe is the biggest problem facing their people today. You should contribute to this part of the test by adding what you believe it is.

ACTION TOMORROW

Spend twenty minutes walking around each section with the member of your team responsible. Stop to talk to every other person. For example, "Say, Suzy, if you were to tell me the biggest problem facing you here at work, what would it be?" Make a quick note of what Suzy says, and then what Maria, Jose, Jack, Mazie, and Pedro say also.

ACTION THE DAY AFTER TOMORROW

Collect your team together and present a collation of your findings. Compare them with the original list. What does the awareness test show?

REMEMBER

The SUPERBOSS never forgets that his people need to be aware too (of what's going on and what he thinks).

··

| **BEHAVIOR** | ## MANAGING PEOPLE SUCCESSFULLY IS ALL TO DO WITH BEHAVIOR. |

A boss's behavior is observed every minute of the working day (and often beyond). It forms the basis upon which people all around judge a person in authority.

Behavior includes the clothes the boss wears and how they are worn. It includes the state of the hair and fingernails. It includes every single word the boss utters and whether or not he or she uses Lagerfield cologne or suffers from body odor. It includes the state of the office and how the boss answers the phone. (You can tell a lot by whether the response is: "Jackie Jones here," or "2348," or "Jones!") It includes the extent to which the boss uses common courtesies, whether excessive rudeness is displayed or the politeness overdone.

Behavior is everything a boss does. It forms the basis for this book. Achievement stems from behavior.

The Superboss is completely conscious of and in command of his behavior. He sets the highest standards of behavior in every respect. He doesn't scowl at the apologetic clerk forcing his way through the door to get an urgent signature, nor does he continually look at his watch when the Employee Relations Manager prattles on. The Superboss never fiddles expenses, nor does he get drunk on formal occasions. He might tell jokes, but they are never offensive. His behavior commands respect, underpins his authority.

The Superboss, even so, knows that he is not perfect, that his behavior cannot always be immaculate. But he always tries to conform to the highest standards, and expects his team to do the same.

ACTION TODAY

Watch your behavior — every minute of the day. Try to be conscious of every eye movement you make when you're with people. Try to control your tendency to sigh, scratch your ear, shake your head, look out of the window. If you want to communicate something to a person, be direct and be polite. It's better to interrupt and say, "I'm afraid I'm going to have to close this meeting in five minutes," rather than continually glance at your watch.

Starting today, discipline yourself to be totally conscious of and in command of your behavior all the time.

REMEMBER
There can be no higher standard of behavior in an organization than that set by a SUPERBOSS.

BELIEFS IF YOU DON'T HAVE SOME BELIEF IN THE RIGHT WAY TO MANAGE, YOU WILL BE TREATED WITH DISBELIEF.

You must have a set of beliefs which forms the basis of all the management action and decisions you take.

In the bad old days you might have held autocratic beliefs. You as a manager had the right to manage and the workforce was there to do what you told them.

Nowadays you might hold more progressive beliefs on participative management. You might spend considerable time with your people consulting them on what has to be done, encouraging them to participate on every issue. Of course, when no one agrees and your boss starts kicking your behind for getting nowhere, you might start questioning your beliefs.

The Superboss has a clear set of management beliefs. He has developed them over a period of years, drawing from his own experience and that of others, learning from his mistakes as well as from training courses and discussions with other management enthusiasts.

He will have evolved a set of values of what he believes to be most important in the process of management. It will be a hierarchy of beliefs which connects people to profit. For example, one of his fundamental beliefs will be that employees should be valued as an asset, not as a cost. From this will stem the belief that a positive, supportive, communicative, co-operative, decisive style of managing people is most likely to produce results.

These beliefs will form the basis of the decisions the Superboss makes, for example with respect to training and development, recruitment, and so on.

The Superboss will have other beliefs within the hierarchical framework, for example with respect to pay, working conditions, and unions.

All together they will form a coherent framework within which the Superboss can manage most effectively. That framework is in fact the framework for this book, the framework for managing people successfully.

ACTION TODAY

Quickly scan some other sections in this book. You will sense a set of underlying management beliefs which the Superboss will have. Do they accord with your own beliefs?

Take one or two of your colleagues for a drink after work today and debate the issue with them. It is of vital importance to you. You must have an effective framework of management beliefs.

QUESTION

Should the SUPERBOSS's beliefs accord with those of his company?

. . . .

BELIEVE TO BELIEVE IN YOUR PEOPLE YOU MUST BELIEVE IN YOURSELF.

Seeing is believing, or so it is said.

The Superboss sees his people working hard, sees them achieving results, sees them putting themselves out.

The Superboss believes in his people because he believes they will do their best for the company, for the department, and for him as well as themselves. They do their best for him because they believe in him, because they believe he will do his best for them.

The Superboss believes in his people because he is proud of them, proud of what they've achieved already, the effort they've put in, and what they'll achieve in the future.

The Superboss shows he believes in them by reflecting what he sees, letting them know he's seen them working hard, achieving results, putting themselves out.

And when his people perform badly or make mistakes he pats them on the back and tells them that he himself is always making mistakes and could do better, that he has made a thousand mistakes in his time. He tells them he still believes in them.

The Superboss believes in his people because he believes in himself. He sees all their weaknesses in himself, as well as their strengths. He believes, in fact knows, that he is forever doing his best. He believes, in fact knows, that his people are also doing their best. If not he would immediately confront the issue. No one will ever admit to not doing their best. If perceptions of "the best" vary, the Superboss will explore that variation with the individual or people concerned.

ACTION TODAY

Ask yourself, "Do my people believe in me?" If you don't know the answer, they probably don't. It's probably because you don't believe in them.

Ask yourself, "Do I believe in every member of my team?"

If not, and there's a person you don't believe in, you have a serious problem. Consult your closest confidant and then call up the person and confront the issue, exploring why you don't think you believe in him or her (i.e., why you don't believe he or she is giving of his or her best). Don't accuse, just discreetly explore the problem. There's no other way you can work.

QUESTION

Do you believe you have a SUPERBOSS? If not, why not? If you believe in yourself, confront the issue and help your boss.

··

Boss NEVER FORGET YOUR BOSS IS A HUMAN BEING TOO.

You might not think it on occasions, but your boss is a human being too. He has feelings, has inner doubts, has problems. Whatever you might believe, your boss thinks about you quite frequently. Your boss is likely to carry more weight on his shoulders than you imagine, and will probably be shielding you from much of it. You might think your boss is indecisive, uncaring, and doesn't understand, but you have to understand that he is subjected to pressures of which you have no perception nor appreciation.

The Superboss is no "creep," but he goes out of his way to help his own boss, never wanting to let him down. He respects his boss's authority and the fact he has probably made it there the hard way. The Superboss will attempt to take as much of the load off his boss's shoulders as possible. He'll volunteer to do things on the boss's behalf. Furthermore, when he presents problems to his boss he ensures they are accompanied by clear-cut recommendations to solve them.

The Superboss is completely loyal to his boss. While he knows the boss is far from perfect, and sometimes inadequate if not incompetent (all bosses appear that way at times), you'll never find the Superboss cutting down his boss behind his back. If the Superboss has any complaints about his boss, he'll take them up with the boss, nobody else, and he'll have an open and honest debate about the issue.

The Superboss works hard for his boss and is wholly committed to what he has to achieve. He never attempts to show his boss up, nor find fault, nor make the person look silly. The Superboss doesn't bear grudges about his boss's failings, nor does he pursue recriminations when his boss makes stupid decisions.

He'll try hard to persuade his boss not to make a certain decision, but if he does the Superboss will accept it gracefully and support it thereafter.

What the Superboss seeks to achieve is an open, honest, supportive, and trusting relationship with his boss.

ACTION TODAY

Be honest and answer these questions:

Do you have any problems with your boss? Have you discussed these problems with him or her? Do you ever attempt to put yourself in your boss's shoes? Is it true you never moan about your boss behind his or her back? Are you completely loyal to him or her? Do you respect your boss?

If your conclusion is that you have a highly imperfect relationship, arrange to see your boss to discuss it. Carefully prepare the answers to the above questions before the meeting. Don't worry about putting your job on the line; an honest approach to solving problems is a thousand times better than sticking your head in the sand and not solving the problem.

If you think your boss is going to fire you for speaking up, you have a serious problem anyway.

REMEMBER

The SUPERBOSS discusses issues with his boss.

BRIEFING   BE BRIEFED, BRIEF, AND BE BRIEF ABOUT IT.

The principle behind briefing groups is great.

The danger is they become just another bureaucratic system substituted for a key management task. Managers will no longer see their task as briefing people, but to issue company briefings.

In one company I knew the senior team spent hours to prepare two-page company briefings to be used down the line. The briefings were invariably full of "gloom and doom" (the Vice President of Finance always making the point that every time we raise expectations with good news "they" will expect a pay increase).

I saw managers pin those briefings on bulletin boards and then pop their heads around the rest room door and scatter a few more copies on the table for the "workers" to read. That was it. That was the briefing.

The company briefing was seen as "management propaganda." The Superboss makes a point first of keeping himself briefed all the time, and then of ensuring that his people are briefed as soon as possible. If the company produces a written briefing, fine; he'll use it to supplement his own briefing. The Superboss knows what interests his people and he briefs them on those subjects. He encourages questions after the briefing and if he doesn't know an answer he'll go and find it. Although the company briefing might refer to an exceptional provision this month for exchange losses, the Superboss will know that his people would prefer to be briefed on when the new forklift trucks are going to be delivered, or when the company is going to renovate their restroom, or when the new warehousing procedure is coming in.

The Superboss keeps his briefings brief. They are always relevant, always face to face, always frequent, and he always provides sufficient time for questions. The Superboss briefs on a regular basis and calls impromptu briefing sessions when necessary.

ACTION TODAY

In you haven't briefed your people personally within the last month you should be fired immediately.

Check your appointment book and allocate sufficient time for briefing sessions over the next four weeks. These should be high priority. Prepare your own briefing carefully, using the most recent company briefing, but concentrating on issues that will interest your people. Allocate sufficient time for questions. Don't just brief your immediate subordinates, go along and contribute to their own briefing sessions down the line.

REMEMBER

People love to be briefed by a SUPERBOSS. It's much better than the grapevine.

CARING   CARE FOR YOUR PEOPLE, THEN TI FOR YOU AND THE COMPANY.

Don't simulate care. If you can't be bothered with your people, don't bother.

The personnel policy for the organization might be "We want to be a people-caring employer," but that means nothing unless every supervisor, manager, and director cares for his or her staff.

The Superboss cares for his people, tries hard to help them with their problems. Furthermore, he shows he cares, shows he is interested in their successes, concerned about their failures. He takes care about their training, development, and career progression. He's careful to give advice and counsel when it's needed.

When things go wrong at home, the Superboss cares enough to see if he can help in any way. He's discreet, but interested. He gives his people time off when they have personal problems and often before they ask. He always takes care to be available.

If anyone is ill he will send a card, some flowers, some magazines—even a bottle of whiskey. His concern is always genuine and he'll even break the rules to show it.

First and foremost however, the Superboss will always drop in to see someone with a problem and ask how things are. He cares that much.

ACTION TODAY

Commit yourself to taking at least one people-caring action today and everyday. It doesn't take too much imagination. For example, find out who's absent or sick and make some positive gesture such as sending a card. This is not a job for the welfare officer; it's a job for you, the Superboss.

Or drop in and see anyone who has just returned to work after a period of illness and show some genuine concern for his or her welfare.

Take an interest today in your people and show you care. They should be very precious to you and you should be proud of them!

REMEMBER

If you care to be a SUPERBOSS, you must care.

CHALLENGE THERE'S NO CHALLENGE LIKE MANAGEMENT.

Climbing Everest, flying to the moon, or writing million-seller books are no bigger challenges than the challenge of management. They are in fact challenges of management. Nobody climbs Everest, gets to the moon, or has a book published by himself. The challenge is the actual process of managing to acquire the desired result.

The physical side (equipment, etc.) is relatively easy. The challenge for the Superboss is two-fold. First, it is identifying the opportunity to achieve something. Second, and much more importantly, it is applying his own skills to developing a superb team to exploit that opportunity. That's the challenge.

Challenges don't come every day, are never routine. They might be a downturn in sales, or a new competitive product, or the sudden resignation of a key person. They might be the introduction of a new electronic mail system, or an urgent order from your biggest customer.

The Superboss loves challenges, seizes them like gold dust, uses them as chances to boost the motivation of his team, to get their adrenaline going, give them excitement. If it means working 18 hours without stopping, then he'll be there too — meeting the challenge with them, working 18 hours without stopping. The Superboss thrives on challenge, and so does his team. And as a result the challenges tend to come his way. People seem to know.

ACTION TODAY

Call your team together over lunch and ask them what sort of thing challenges them. Also ask what they see as the biggest challenge facing them over the coming months.

Discuss with them how they're going to meet that challenge.

You'll feel much better afterwards, and so will they. That's the challenge!

QUESTION
Who challenges the SUPERBOSS?

CHANGE | PROGRESS IS SYNONYMOUS WITH CHANGE.

If nothing ever changes in an organization then it becomes an exceedingly boring place. Its products become dowdy, its services dated, its environment dreary, its machinery dilapidated, and its people deadly dull.

Dull and dreary people resist change. They feel secure in the comfort of what they already know. Change frightens them, whether it be a new computer system, a new boss or a new office to work in.

The Superboss knows that there is no alternative to change. The environment is changing all the time (new markets, new governments, new attitudes) while the competition always seems to be racing ahead. There are always pressures for more efficient working practices, for new technology, for new products, for new sales campaigns, and even for new people.

The Superboss thrives on change, loves it. It keeps his adrenaline going and gives him the constant satisfaction of challenge in his job. But he recognizes the fears his people have, the insecurity they feel. So he spends a lot of time with them, explaining and discussing the need for change, reassuring them, attempting to excite their interest. He persuades them that a change to a new electronic mail system is absolutely necessary; that pay anomalies are such that there is no option but to change to a new job evaluation system; that shortage of space really does mean a move to a new office across the road. The Superboss persuades them that a change to reduced employee levels must take place now that automated packaging has come in, reassuring them at the same time that natural attrition will take care of the reduction.

Whatever the change the Superboss takes care to do the right thing by his people, the best he can for them. He'll never rush change, spending an enormous amount of time consulting his people about it, attempting to take them along with him, gaining their consent and cooperation.

The last thing a Superboss wants to do is impose change, but sometimes it is the last thing he has to do.

ACTION TODAY

Walk around your area and ask each person you meet, "If there's one change you would like to see here, what would it be?" Review your findings with your immediate subordinates and draw up a plan to make the agreed changes. Then go back to the people who wanted the change and advise them of your plans.

QUESTION

Who can change a SUPERBOSS?

CHARACTER — THE CHARACTER OF THE MANAGER IS REFLECTED IN THE CHARACTER OF HIS TEAM.

Character-less is colorless. Character-less is having no personality, no life, no excitement, no interests, no energy. I've met character-less managers who sit there day by day, pushing papers around, waiting for problems to reach their desk and then deflecting them on to someone else. If such managers do have character it is but to moan and groan and criticize everyone else: their bosses, their colleagues, and even their subordinates.

To be character-less as a manager is to be negative in the extreme.

The Superboss has character, is a character. His character shows in the way he deals with people, his boss, his staff, his colleagues. It shows in how he handles situations and the problems that come his way. It shows in the little eccentricities people love him for. His character gives color to their everyday working lives.

The color of the Superboss's character shows through. It bears a distinctive mark which people see and talk about. "One thing you've got to learn about Joe," people will say to a new member of their team about their Superboss, "is keep out of his way on Monday morning; that's the only time he'll ever snap at you. Always see him after lunch if you want anything." In another department it might be, "I'll tell you about Frank, he's a great boss, but you won't get to know him until you've had your first argument. Be prepared for it, it will be some experience, but after that you'll have his total confidence and support."

The character of the Superboss will be reflected in the character of his team because they will reflect his values, his beliefs. What is important for him will be important for them.

ACTION TODAY

Write this at the back of your appointment book: *"From now on I will never ever undertake any character assassination: boss, senior executive, chief executive, subordinate, colleague, or acquaintance."*

Then think about ways of developing your own character and the character of your team. To be a Superboss your character must have a positive distinctive mark. What is it?

Check on it. Take your personnel manager into your confidence and ask for help in giving some feedback on how people see your character.

REMEMBER

The SUPERBOSS characterizes all that is best in the company.

CHIEF EXECUTIVE

IF THE CHIEF EXECUTIVE IS NOT A SUPERBOSS FEW OTHERS IN THE ORGANIZATION WILL BE.

The worrisome thing is that many Chief Executives are not Superbosses. They might be excellent at financial control, acquisition strategy, long-term planning, commercial wheeling and dealing. What they are less good at is being a Superboss. Such Chief Executives tend to give low priority to people issues and even lower priority to the critical task of developing leadership and management capability.

If Chief Executives believe that the only way to achieve profit through people is to have as many Superbosses in the organization as possible, then they have to be Superbosses themselves. They have to set the example, demonstrate a style of leadership which other senior executives will follow. It's no good Chief Executives encouraging managers to "walk about and be visible" if they rarely do it themselves. It's no good Chief Executives issuing policy directives (written by personnel people) making performance appraisal mandatory — and then not carrying out appraisals themselves. It's no good Chief Executives saying that management development and training are essential and then cutting back on the management training budget.

The Chief Executive who is a Superboss will delegate many of the non-people-oriented tasks, devoting as much time as possible to developing a top team of Superbosses and helping them build their own teams. The Chief Executive will also get round the organization and meet as many people as possible. He will have a clear-cut philosophy on how to manage people successfully and will always try to adopt and practice this throughout the organization.

The Chief Executive who is a Superboss will be applying most of what is referred to in this book, knowing that as the company's leader only he can create an environment, a climate in which other Superbosses can thrive.

ACTION TODAY

If you're a Chief Executive, commission a consultant to undertake a climate survey among all your managers and determine whether or not you are a Superboss. You might just be surprised at how the findings correlate with your company results.

REMEMBER

To be a super company with super results the Chief Executive must be a SUPERBOSS.

CLARITY — WOULD YOU DRIVE A CAR WITHOUT CLEAR VISION?

Autocratic managers are very bad at this, especially egocentric Chairmen. They issue instructions which nobody understands and which nobody dares question. The autocrats automatically assume that because they themselves understand, others will. Everyone rushes around trying to carry out the instruction knowing full well they'll be reprimanded for making the wrong assumptions about what the Chairman wanted. C'est la vie!

The Superboss is very clear about what the company wants of him and very clear about how he's going to achieve it. What's more, he makes sure his people are clear too. He chooses his words carefully, doesn't use loose terminology. He doesn't make ambiguous statements nor dither over a decision he finds difficult to make. He spells out what he wants and then checks with his people that they understand.

Conversely, when his people bring a problem to him, he ensures he is 100 percent clear about it. He doesn't make any assumptions until he achieves this clarity, questioning them thoroughly to make sure.

ACTION TODAY

At 9:30 prompt this evening stop whatever you're doing, make your wife (husband, partner) a large mug of hot chocolate and invite her (him) to participate in a simulated workplace experiment. Switch on the cassette recorder.

You are allowed five minutes to explain the most important things you are doing at work at the moment. A further five minutes is allowed for questions of clarification.

Now turn off the cassette recorder, turn the television back on and drink your hot chocolate.

ACTION TOMORROW

At 9:30 prompt tomorrow evening get your partner to stop whatever he or she is doing and make you a mug of hot chocolate. Turn on the cassette recorder and ask your partner to repeat what you told her or him yesterday.

Compare the two cassette recordings. If there's 100 percent repetition then not only are you a super clear boss, but you have a super partner. (Why should your partner be less clear about those important things at work than someone on the factory floor who works for you?)

REMEMBER

The SUPERBOSS knows that without clarity there are clouds of every shape and form.

CLIMATE — EVERY ACTION A LEADER TAKES, EVERY DECISION HE MAKES, WILL HAVE A DIRECT IMPACT ON THE CLIMATE IN HIS ORGANIZATION.

Climate is how people feel about their boss and how they feel about the company. It can be hot, cold, stormy, sticky, warm, or many other things. It can be a clear climate too.

Poor bosses give no time to their people, neglect them while pursuing "more important" matters such as financial planning, sales campaigns, engineering reviews, or overseas trips. Their neglect will create a poor climate in their department, morale will be low, people will become less motivated. Their neglect will lead at times to a confusion about what they have to do, to a lack of resolution of daily problems. It will lead to a feeling that their contribution is not being recognized and to a dissipation of team spirit.

The Superboss aims to develop a warm, supportive, cooperative climate where high standards are accepted and expected, where the team's objectives are crystal clear. The climate the Superboss seeks to create is one where every employee is totally committed to the company's goals and works hard to contribute towards them.

The Superboss therefore spends considerable time developing this climate, ensuring that people are clear about what is required of them, that their contribution is recognized, and that the team is working well together.

He will frequently test the climate, sometimes directly by getting a group together and checking on a number of climate factors, sometimes informally by just strolling around and chatting with people. The Superboss can sense the climate in an office or on the factory floor by the way the people are working, the way they behave towards each other, towards their boss as well as him. He can sense it by whether they smile or joke, or whether they look downright miserable. He can sense it from the degree of interest shown by the people in what he has to say, or by their moaning and groaning, or by their aggression.

ACTION TODAY
Check three key climate factors:
(a) Is everybody clear about what they're doing?
(b) Do they feel their contribution is recognized?
(c) Do they work well together as a team?

Ask your Organization Development expert, whether he be a consultant or a Human Resources specialist, to survey the climate. Do it informally at first, but if there is a problem commission a more formal survey. Give careful attention to the findings, and don't stick your head in the sand. Don't forget that you are the biggest influence on the climate in your area.

REMEMBER
For a SUPERBOSS climate is a key determinant of performance.

COMMITMENT

COMMITMENT DOESN'T GUARANTEE SUCCESS, BUT LACK OF IT GUARANTEES FAILURE.

I've come across a thousand managers who lack backbone—all experts in telling you the problem, but not in committing to you that they'll find a solution.

Commitment requires courage and taking risks. It means giving your all to other people, totally identifying with their goals. Commitment cannot be imposed by the company. It is something that is self-generated, based on one's own internal convictions.

Managers who lack backbone cover their options, duck and weave to avoid commitment. They'll talk forever rather than be pinned down. They're all too familiar. All words but no committed action. They would rather let you down tomorrow than commit to you today.

People respect a Superboss because he's prepared to commit to them. He's prepared to commit to his boss to producing an extra 4 percent output next week, or getting that new plant commissioned within three months. He's prepared to commit to his people. He's prepared to commit that a new air-conditioning unit will be installed, or that a problem with travel allowances will be resolved. When the Superboss commits to a person to do something he will do it.

However, you will never find the Superboss committing to something he knows is impossible to achieve. He'll take a risk if there's an element of doubt, but if he's convinced it's impossible he won't commit. But that is rare. The Superboss demonstrates the art of the possible, achieving results which other managers may say are impossible. (How else could you get to the moon?)

ACTION TODAY

List your commitments to others — your colleagues, your boss, your people. If you don't have any commitments, you and your company have a serious problem.

Check the list to ensure you've honored each commitment. If not, make sure you do.

From now on, as a managerial discipline, whenever you're asked for a decision, or to pursue a line of action, make a commitment to the person who's asking. You must mean it, and you must follow through. If you don't trust yourself to remember, make a note of your commitment.

REMEMBER

The SUPERBOSS always commits to the person. The evidence of his commitment is his action, not his words.

COMMUNICATION

COMMUNICATION IS NOT THE PANACEA FOR ALL EMPLOYEE RELATIONS PROBLEMS.

It is naiveté of the highest order to assume that if you shovel more information down the organization pipeline your employee relations problems will disappear. Yet I have seen such naiveté at the highest levels. It is the assumption that if you tell your employees what the company's problems are, if you tell them "the facts," they will understand. Which is, of course, what they manifestly fail to do. Always.

In organizations rife with distrust, top-down communication campaigns will always be perceived by employees as company propaganda and brain washing. Employees will be suspicious of the catch. "They're trying to con us once more," they will say, or "they're trying to soften us up again."

To communicate effectively you must have trust. To achieve trust you must create an environment in which your employees can genuinely communicate with you, and you must genuinely listen and take the appropriate follow-through action.

When it comes to communication therefore the Superboss starts at the other end. He allows his people to communicate with him, allows them to ask questions on issues which interest them. He devotes time to it. If they're interested in remittances from Nigeria then he'll tell them, but he won't force it down reluctant throats.

However, actions speak louder than words. You can have all the communications you like, but unless you take action nobody will believe the communication. The danger is the "cry wolf" syndrome, or the "mañana" mentality.

In communicating, the Superboss never says anything he doesn't believe or doesn't mean. He would not say, for example, "Unless we cut costs by 10 percent the company will go out of business," unless he was convinced that it would. His communications carry conviction and that's why his people believe and trust him. Furthermore, when they communicate to him they know he will genuinely listen, and will try to follow through with any appropriate action.

ACTION TODAY

Go down to the canteen at coffee break, or wander along to the office water cooler. Chat with your people about communications within the company and how they might be improved. Listen carefully to what they have to say and follow up with any agreed action.

Be prepared for complaints like, "We always find out through the grapevine." (How are you going to be more effective than the grapevine?)

ACTION NEXT WEEK

Discipline yourself to plan all formal communications very carefully. If you're about to introduce an important organization change, spend half a day thinking about the best way to communicate it, making sure the right people know at the right time.

Don't let the grapevine take over. It will distort things and reduce your credibility.

REMEMBER

The SUPERBOSS devotes over 80 percent of his time to communications. He is the company when it comes to company communications.

COMPASSION — MANAGING PEOPLE IS A CROSS BETWEEN COMPASSION AND COMPETITION.

A feeling is a fact. Everybody has feelings. Some show them, others suppress them.

One of the key skills in management is to identify and recognize the other person's feelings. If they are negative (shame, guilt, inadequacy, loss of face, helplessness, rejection, embarrassment, self-doubt), help transform them into something more positive (pride, confidence, satisfaction, acceptance, joy, elation, goodwill).

The degree to which a manager can identify with the other person's feelings is the degree of compassion he or she will have. The manager who neglects people's feelings does so at his or her peril. That manager will be shown to be a person who has no compassion, is ruthless, self-seeking, and who treats people like machines.

The Superboss feels for his people. He shows compassion when Hank Delale has to go into the hospital for a varicose vein operation. He shows compassion when young Sandra MacLellan is shouted down by an aggressive teammate. He shows compassion when Meg Chaucer fails her accountancy exams. He shows compassion when his boss is made to look stupid in front of him.

The Superboss exercises compassion by trying to help the person eliminate those negative feelings. He tries to inject warmth, encouragement, support, and help into the situation to alleviate the problem and give the person confidence. He will reassure Hank Delale about the skill of the surgeons, reassure him that his job will be kept open for him as long as need be. He will soothe Sandra MacLellan and tell her that in his view she had a good point. He will tell Meg Chaucer that you don't always win first time, and will encourage her to try again.

But there are always losers, and the Superboss has compassion for them too. He has compassion for the people he occasionally has to dismiss, the people who lose a relative, or suffer permanent disability. He doesn't raise their hopes, in no way is he false. But the Superboss will do everything to help in these situations.

ACTION TODAY

Ask yourself, when dealing with any person today: "How does that person feel?" You won't always know, but you might be able to find out. You might be able to demonstrate some compassion and be able to help. Always put yourself in the other person's shoes and show some compassion.

REMEMBER

Show your SUPERBOSS some compassion; he has feelings too.

COMPETITION — MANAGING PEOPLE IS A CROSS BETWEEN COMPETITION AND COMPASSION.

Competition should be a spur to improvement. However, in any competition there are rules relating to morality, law, ethics, and, if it's internal competition, company policy.

The Superboss encourages competition. He encourages his team to win each round and get to the top of the league. He encourages open competition, abhors behind-the-back political competition. If he's managing the night shift, the Superboss will encourage his team to produce more than the afternoon or morning shift. He'll encourage them to achieve higher quality ratings. If he's the Regional Sales Manager, he'll encourage his team to beat the sales levels of all other regions.

The Superboss also encourages his team to compete against themselves, for example to beat last month's production record or exceed last month's revenue figures.

He encourages individual competition too, for example as "employee of the month" in service environments. Even so he'll ensure it's fair competition and that everyone has an equal opportunity to compete.

At a different level the Superboss will encourage his people to compete for promotion to other departments, for career development opportunities, and for the highest scores on training courses. He knows that for his company to survive in a harsh competitive world he needs to encourage a competitive spirit among all his people.

However, in encouraging competition the Superboss will protect his team, will not allow anyone to ride roughshod over them, nor will he allow any individual to be sacrificed or destroyed in the process. Competition can only be healthy if it's combined with compassion. That's the balance between profit and people.

ACTION TODAY

Set two types of competition.

1. A simple competition whereby your team can compete with another team in the company. (Don't be negative. There are even ways in which one accounts section can compete with another.) Consult your team on how to do this.

2. An individual competition between all the people in your division or department. If you've no idea at all how to do this, consult your people. They might suggest, for example, the best time-keeping competition; the best attendance record; the individual who smiles the most; the individual who moans the least. What about a general knowledge quiz about the company?

REMEMBER

For the SUPERBOSS competition not only leads to success, but makes for great fun at work.

CONFLICT — CONFLICT SHOULD ALWAYS BE ON THE SURFACE, NEVER BENEATH.

The Superboss brings conflict to the surface. There it can be examined, studied, and resolved.

The Superboss will sense the conflict. He might not see it at first, but he'll feel it bubbling, festering under the surface. He'll feel it by the way people talk, by certain snide comments, by frequent cutting remarks, by a stream of obnoxious little memos. Sometimes the issue will be big, for example, a conflict over a pay differential between two sections. At other times it will be relatively small, such as some personal animosity between two members of the team.

As soon as he senses the conflict the Superboss will bring it to the surface. He'll try to get the facts and then at the root cause of the problem. He'll bring together the protagonists around the table and open up with them. "I could be wrong," he might say, "but I sense we have some little problem brewing over the proposed transfer to Chapel House."

When the conflict is exposed he'll keep the protagonists talking until everyone agrees on a solution. If that's not possible he'll get them to agree he should arbitrate and that his decision will be final.

Sometimes the Superboss has his own internal conflicts, for example when he believes the company is acting unwisely. He'll discuss them with his boss and try to keep an open mind. Unless he persuades his boss otherwise, he will ultimately have to accept the company's decision. If a conflict of conscience remains, he has only one option—that is to resign. And the Superboss will, and the company knows it. It rarely happens, because the Superboss thrives best where his principles accord with the company's.

ACTION TODAY

Think deeply about what's been going on in your department recently. Be completely honest with yourself (don't stick your head in the sand). Do you sense any areas of conflict or potential conflict? If so, call your team together and discuss your concern.

Bring the issue to the surface and get their views, not only on the perceived conflict but how to resolve it. Then resolve it.

REMEMBER

When the SUPERBOSS is around there's little conflict.

CONSENT — TO MANAGE BY CONSENT IS NOT TO ABDICATE ONE'S RESPONSIBILITY, BUT TO STRENGTHEN ONE'S AUTHORITY.

There is a myth among certain hard-nosed autocratic managers that to manage by consent is to be soft.

The fact is that to manage by consent is very hard and the only way any leader can get people to follow along.

Consent concerns the exercise and acceptance of reason. The Superboss is reasonable and demonstrates it. Before he makes a decision, he'll attempt to gain a consensus by consulting his people. Having made a decision, he'll give reasons for it. Sometimes his decision will go against a certain group of people, but they will consent to it knowing that he has given them a proper hearing with careful consideration to their views, that he has exercised his authority in a fair and objective way, and that he had to make a decision which could go against them.

To gain consent the Superboss spends a lot of time with his people, explaining the complexities of the situation and the many contradictory factors influencing the final decision. He will seek their views and give a lot of weight to them. He will put himself in their shoes with respect to any issue affecting them. Similarly, he will ask them to put themselves in his shoes with respect to the decisions he has to make.

The Superboss knows that management by consent is not the same as management by permission. Never would he go to the union and ask permission for a change in personnel arrangements, nor would he go to his people and ask permission to install a new piece of machinery. He will seek their consent, but in the end he knows the decision will have to be his, for only he has the authority to make that decision, and only he carries accountability for it.

ACTION TODAY

Cast your mind back over some important decisions you've made recently which have had an impact on your people. Can you honestly say you sought their consent? Can you honestly say that they are behind you? If any decision went against your people's views, can you honestly say you went out of your way to explain why?

ACTION IN THE FUTURE

Discipline yourself to delay any decisions affecting your people until you've had an opportunity to gauge their views and seek their consent. But remember, seeking consent is not asking permission.

REMEMBER

Although the SUPERBOSS will always seek consent, he knows that it is rare that everyone will agree with his final decision.

CONSIDERATION

TO GIVE GENUINE CONSIDERATION YOU MUST ALWAYS PUT YOURSELF IN THE OTHER PERSON'S SHOES.

I've met many managers who lack consideration for the people with whom they deal. They'll cut people short, not giving them a chance to open their mouths. They will pour scorn on others' ideas, making people look small. They'll neither listen nor pay attention when someone else is speaking. They'll turn up late for meetings, frequently jerking people around and letting them down.

Never the Superboss. He listens, he considers. He always puts himself in the other person's shoes and starts from there. He tries to understand how the person feels when talking to him.

He gives consideration to every individual he deals with because he respects that that person will have something important to say and furthermore will need to preserve an inner dignity, will need to maintain face in his eyes. The Superboss is so considerate he will never deliberately make another person look or feel small.

Giving consideration is not just a matter of showing humility, it's also a matter of finding and giving time to the person with the problem. The Superboss always finds the time for people. In a meeting, whether it be with one person or fifteen you won't see the Superboss dismissing a person's statement with his eyes; you won't see him frowning or showing signs of irritability when someone else opens his mouth and comes up with a crazy idea. The Superboss will consider all points of view. He'll encourage others to speak and then listen attentively, concentrating on what is being said, and giving it genuine consideration.

ACTION TODAY

Hold yourself back. Whoever comes into your office, let them do the talking. Say little, encourage them to talk, and listen carefully.

Put yourself in that person's shoes and consider their feelings and what they are saying.

Always assume that their motives are honest and that they are trying to say something important and furthermore trying to help the company. Never dismiss that contribution. Consider it and value it.

REMEMBER

The SUPERBOSS spends more time considering his people than considering himself.

 ## TO HAVE THE COURSE OF YOUR MANAGEMENT CONVICTIONS YOU MUST BE PREPARED TO PUT YOUR JOB ON THE LINE.

This is the big test. This is when managers duck below the parapet and look the other way, or don't speak up when an injustice is being perpetrated by the company. This is when you disagree violently with your boss and then vindictively try to sabotage his plans behind his or her back. This is when you stick your head in the sand and do nothing when that disruptive Billy Murphy starts stirring up trouble again.

This is when you prefer to patch a festering little problem, rather than take the more painful action to prevent the longer term crisis.

The Superboss has the courage of his convictions. It gives him strength and the senior hierarchy knows it.

The Superboss will speak up when he sees an injustice being perpetrated, when he feels Pam Alton is not being given a fair hearing by Public Affairs, or when Steve Malek starts behaving vindictively towards Angela Long, one of his juniors. The Superboss, if he vehemently disagrees with his own boss will confront him and have the matter out. If it's a major issue he'll either be persuaded or resign.

ACTION TODAY

Go home tonight and have a hypothetical discussion with your wife, husband, or partner. Discuss at what stage you would be prepared to put your job on the line. Think carefully; you have a family and financial commitments. You know that other jobs aren't that easy to come by. Do you really have the courage of your own convictions?

Or are you one of those spineless creatures that float around large organizations like jellyfish, stinging other people but doing little else? Think of situations where you might have to put your job on the line. Would you? Would you? Would you?

REMEMBER

You can't become a SUPERBOSS without the courage of your convictions.

COOPERATION — IS THERE ANY OTHER WAY BUT TO WORK TOGETHER AND COOPERATE?

The only alternative to working together is working against. When someone is working against you it is not always obvious. Things take a little longer to get done, but you're not sure why. People forget to do things. More often than not lack of cooperation shows up through lethargy, through not being bothered, through lack of interest. Others will not put themselves out for you.

People don't cooperate because they're not with you. More than likely they're not with you because they don't think you're with them. "Why should I bother with him? He doesn't bother with me except when he wants something."

The Superboss seeks cooperation and gets it. He gets it because he's with his people, not just in the task that has to be performed today, but in pursuing their interests, supporting them, putting himself out for them. The Superboss co-operates with his people in helping resolve their problems, and in return they cooperate with him. It's a two-way process, each side putting itself out for the other. You can't expect people to cooperate with you if you don't cooperate with them.

The Superboss therefore always sets the example and takes the initiative in cooperating. He doesn't wait until he wants something and then ask for cooperation. If Tony Kidd wants his help in presenting a prize he'll cooperate. If Jessica Landor wants him to write a reference to the bank he'll cooperate. If his boss wants him to show a visiting Japanese delegation around he'll cooperate. In cooperating the Superboss will always show willingness; he'll never throw up excuses and pretend it's all too difficult. He'll go out of his way to cooperate, to help the other person with whatever he or she wants.

ACTION TODAY

Make a list of the twenty people with whom you have to work most closely. Then rank them in order of cooperativeness. Forget the top ten, they're not a problem. Now look critically at the ten who are least cooperative and ask yourself why. If your answers are all to do with them, take another look at the lower list and ask yourself, "Is their lack of cooperativeness perhaps because they don't think I cooperate with them?" Be ruthlessly self-critical; you might learn a lot and help yourself, and them.

REMEMBER

Many people cooperated to make him the SUPERBOSS he is.

COUNSELING NO MANAGER CAN BE HIS OWN COUNSELOR.

Contemplating one's own navel is fine and very necessary at times. However, one's navel is not equipped to provide excellent counsel, which we all need on occasion.

Excellent counsel should always be aimed at helping the individual. For once profit and the company should be forgotten. When the Superboss sits down to counsel someone he only has one interest in mind — to help that person. He'll try to see the problem from his or her point of view. He might also hold up a mirror to the face, trying to reflect how the issue is seen in the eyes of others. By getting different perspectives the Superboss attempts to focus in on the problem.

Having held up the mirror he'll encourage the other person to talk further about the problem, even to suggest solutions. Only then will the Superboss offer his own advice, for what it is worth. The Superboss also seeks counsel frequently. He will turn to his boss for guidance and advice. There will be one or two of his colleagues whose counsel he values greatly.

The Superboss also takes counsel from his subordinates, knowing that in many areas they have greater wisdom, insight, and experience of the type of problem on which he needs help.

ACTION TODAY

Set up a series of person-to-person counsel meetings with individuals you know in your area (not just your direct subordinates). The purpose of the meeting is to focus on each person's specific interests (i.e., career interests, job interests, other work-related interests). Prepare carefully for each meeting. Think only of the person you're going to counsel and try to identify his or her specific needs and problem areas. At the counsel meeting be as relaxed, warm, and informal as possible. You should try to generate a constructive atmosphere. You are there to help that person.

Anything he or she says to you should not be used in evidence against him or her.

REMEMBER
Always take counsel from a SUPERBOSS.

CREATIVITY — IT DOESN'T TAKE MUCH IMAGINATION TO BE CREATIVE.

In the most exciting companies creative management is at the forefront. Each supervisor, manager, and senior executive will be creative, whatever the job or situation.

The process of giving birth to new ideas and pursuing them to implementation is one of the most exhilarating aspects of management.

Opportunities for creative management exist all the time. Any organization that seeks to stifle creativity will eventually stifle its own further success because outside its walls is a dynamic competitive world which is forever changing, forever threatening, forever challenging, and forever requiring a creative response. Creative managers thrive on these dynamics. The whole process of getting a superb team of people behind you requires the highest creative skills. It requires creative skills to communicate effectively, to reward people fairly, to stimulate others to even higher standards of performance, and to fight the competition.

The Superboss is creative and encourages creativity. He is always seeking new ways of getting his team to work cohesively and effectively to meet daily challenges. He'll encourage his people to come up with new ideas and help find ways of pursuing them. It might be a new way of charting production output hour by hour; or a new hot-line company communication system; or a new service to the customer. It might be anything that helps the company achieve even more profit.

ACTION TODAY

Think of an idea for encouraging creativity among your people. Here's a suggestion: establish a bi-monthly creativity session from a selection of staff at all levels in your area. Each session should last for two hours.

Divide the group (maximum 12 people) into two teams and put them into separate rooms. Each team should nominate a leader. For the first 45 minutes each team should brainstorm and then prioritize creative ideas for improvement in your area. During the next 15 minutes each team should briefly present their top two priority creative ideas to the other team.

For the next 45 minutes they should evaluate the feasibility of the other's creative ideas. The last 15 minutes should be spent briefly presenting the four evaluations.

You, as boss, then have to decide which of the four creative ideas you are going to pursue and implement (you can choose one, two, three, or four of the ideas, but at least one). You must give your commitment to pursue the idea.

REMEMBER

For the SUPERBOSS it's creativity that helps create profit.

 **IT CAN TAKE ONE MINUTE AND ONE DECISION FOR A MANAGER TO LOSE CREDIBILITY. IT WILL TAKE YEARS AND A THOUSAND DECISIONS FOR THAT MANAGER TO REGAIN IT.**

Expediency is not compatible with credibility, yet many managers I have come across are expedient. They take the easy way out of a difficulty; an easy way out that is neither compatible with the long-term aims of the organization, nor with what that manager has been saying these last few months.

Expediency results from a lack of backbone, a lack of clear thinking, a lack of an effective management philosophy, a lack of sincerity. Expediency leads to a loss of credibility in managers. They become "all things to all people." Their staff begin to run rings around them and the unions exploit the situation further. Their bosses and colleagues see them as a soft option and take advantage whenever they can.

To be an effective manager you must have credibility in the eyes of your boss, your colleagues, and your people. The Superboss achieves credibility by being totally consistent, fair, and firm. The Superboss achieves credibility because when he says something his people know he means it and he'll do what he says.

The Superboss achieves credibility because other people know exactly where they stand with him, because he is wholly predictable and reliable. You will never find a Superboss changing his arguments to suit his case, nor inventing reasons to justify a decision that has been made. The Superboss puts his money where his mouth is, so to speak. He is sincere. The credibility of the Superboss gives his people a sense of security, of well-being. They know he will do his best for them. They know that he will only make painful decisions as a last resort and to that extent they will accept those decisions, trusting him. The manager who lacks credibility will find it nigh impossible to make painful decisions.

Any attempt to do so will be fought every inch of the way, and more than likely he will back down.

ACTION TODAY

Don't eat anything at lunchtime. Let your stomach give you a little gnawing pain (it won't hurt you, millions are starving and experience far worse). Walk for half an hour taking the most scenic route, or drive to a park and walk for half an hour. Take a deep breath and think very deeply and very honestly. Ask yourself the question, "Do I have credibility in the eyes of the people around me?" You should be able to collect together in your mind a large number of clues and cues which indicate your degree of credibility. Compare, for example, the number of times people aggressively challenge your ideas and decisions as opposed to coming to you to seek advice. If you are not sure about your credibility rating you undoubtedly have a credibility problem. Start the long haul this afternoon.

REMEMBER

The SUPERBOSS achieves credibility by turning words into results.

DECISIVENESS — To DECIDE IS TO MANAGE.

The Superboss has an affinity for decisions. He loves making them and seizes every opportunity to do so. His biggest danger is that he oversteps the mark and starts making other people's decisions.

He makes decisions virtually every minute of the working day — decisions whether or not to visit the Head Office on Friday, to pop down at 10:30 for a quick coffee with Mike Appleyard, to raise last week's quality problem at the next team meeting, to send Joni Pollard on a special three-day training course.

But every decision the Superboss makes is directed towards two things. What is right for the company in terms of profit? And what is right for his people? If he's not clear he'll ask for more information, give the matter some further thought, consult a few people (his boss, employee representatives, and others). Then, when he's clear about the impact on people and profit, he'll make a decision.

The real test for the Superboss, however, is whether or not he can make painful decisions, for example the occasional but necessary dismissal, or a layoff.

The Superboss is prepared to suffer pain in deciding what's best for the company and its people.

ACTION TODAY

You've probably been making more decisions per square foot of office space than you'd ever realized. So first of all just list the decisions you made yesterday, small or big. Study each one and question how it impacted profit and people. If you can't answer that, why on earth did you make a decision?

When you've finished studying this list prepare a second one. This should include all the issues on which you did not make a decision yesterday. Study this second list and ask yourself what the consequences were of not making a decision. Can you honestly say there were no negative consequences, for example wasting more of your over-worked boss's time by asking him to make the decision for you, or alienating your people further with your indecisive procrastination? If your study does reveal some negative impact from your indecisiveness, reverse the situation immediately. Be positive, make a decision now.

REMEMBER

The SUPERBOSS always has a reason for his decisions. The reason is profit and people.

DELEGATION

DELEGATION IS THE DISCOVERY THAT YOUR PEOPLE ARE 100 PERCENT MORE CAPABLE THAN YOU'D EVER REALIZED.

You think you know it all. After all, you were promoted and they weren't. You know best. You want to make all the decisions. You're not confident your people understand; not confident they will do as good a job as you. Isn't it easier and faster to do it yourself, to make the decisions? No! Because you're a Superboss.

The fact is each member of your team spends most of his or her time on the job and is more expert at it than you'd ever think. The people doing the job tend to know best about it. If they think they can do better then they might seek your advice, but don't force it down their throats.

The Superboss lets his team get on with the job. He trusts them. He delegates all decisions about the job to them. Even so, he tends to be around most of the time in case they need him. He shows an interest but doesn't interfere. The Superboss knows that if he interferes he may as well do their job, in which case they can sit back, relax, and put their feet on the table. (In badly run companies this is called inefficiency.)

ACTION TODAY

Question every decision you have to make today. Could it be made by one of your people? If so, refer it back and say: "I think that's your decision; I trust you'll make the right one. If you need my help let me know." Push as many of these decisions down as possible.

Furthermore, just check today that every person in your team knows what he or she has to achieve in terms of business results. Then sit back and let them achieve it, encouraging them to make the appropriate decisions en route.

ACTION NEXT WEEK

Take the next two weeks off, delegating everything to your people, and discover how capable they are. Tell your boss you're attending a self-funded experiential self-training course on delegation at some hotel by the sea.

REMEMBER

The SUPERBOSS is as good as the decisions his people make, but no good at all if they don't make any.

DEVELOPMENT — THE KEY TO EMPLOYEE DEVELOPMENT IS BOTH PERSONAL INTEREST BY THE EMPLOYEE'S MANAGER AND SELF-INTEREST BY THE EMPLOYEE.

You can't impose development on an individual; he or she has to want it.

The Superboss knows that employee development is most effective when he takes a personal interest and gives it a lot of time. The Superboss will hold informal discussions with as many of his people as possible about their aspirations and development needs. He'll go to Personnel and take their advice about the best career move, say for Tess Weller or Stan Bishop.

The Superboss is prepared to lose his best people in developing them, encouraging them to transfer to other departments to gain vital experience and to apply for promotion out of his area. In addition to individual meetings the Superboss will sit down with his immediate team and rigorously review development opportunities for their more junior staff. They will always follow up with the agreed action.

The Superboss will encourage new recruits to develop by studying for professional qualifications, giving them time off for it, and even paying their fees.

The Superboss does all this and much more. He gets a great thrill out of seeing his people develop their careers and move on to take more senior positions. He will have a reputation for providing an excellent training and development ground for the up and coming "stars" in the organization. To a certain extent people working for the Superboss will be seen as "elite," people who are going places. He sets high standards of performance and pushes his people to achieve them, thus creating opportunities to demonstrate their skills and giving them beneficial development experience.

The Superboss never holds his people down, is always encouraging them to develop. But he's honest enough to talk bluntly to those who have unrealistic career aspirations, who expect promotions within six months. He'll tell them to demonstrate some achievement over the next two years, then he might consider a career move for them.

ACTION TODAY

Plan to sit down with your team and systematically review everybody in the division, discussing their development and potential. Ask the Personnel Officer to attend, so that he or she can help you make progress on the actions agreed. You must follow through and implement these actions.

QUESTION

How do you develop to become a SUPERBOSS?

DISCIPLINE — THE LEADER WHO HAS EFFECTIVE DISCIPLINE IN HIS OR HER TEAM WILL NEVER NEED TO DISCIPLINE ANYONE.

Without discipline, standards will erode. More people will arrive late for work, take extended lunch breaks, use company stationery for personal purposes, make private calls on the company telephone and "expand" on expenses. And that's just at a personal level.

Company standards will also erode. Equipment will not be maintained, facilities not cleaned adequately, air-conditioning units not repaired. Customer service will deteriorate and profit will fall. The Superboss believes in self-discipline. He applies it to himself and encourages his team to show it. From time to time he will review discipline in the department, looking at the degree to which standards are being maintained and the degree to which people accept and apply them. But he doesn't only review the discipline exercised by his people, he also reviews the company's own discipline in looking after its people.

The Superboss knows that discipline disappears when people feel the company is exploiting them. The company takes them for granted. That's when the people start exploiting the company: unofficial perks will proliferate, petty thieving will become endemic, corrupt practices will become the way of life.

The Superboss disciplines himself never to do anything which will be perceived by his people as exploiting them. Conversely he doesn't tolerate his people exploiting the company. He doesn't tolerate casual breaking of the rules, or lowering the standard of the enterprise. He quietly makes sure they all know the rules, explaining that they are there for a purpose, a good purpose.

The Superboss doesn't have people in his team who are deliberately going to break those rules. Everyone knows that the Superboss will severely discipline a person who transgresses. But in the Superboss's area this rarely happens.

ACTION TODAY

Put on the agenda for your next team meeting "review of department discipline." At that meeting quietly ensure that your people
are clear about the discipline standards required and that they are
accepted and applied.

REMEMBER

The SUPERBOSS believes in discipline, but is not a disciplinarian.

DISMISSAL DISMISSAL IS AN ADMISSION OF COMPANY FAILURE.

Dismissal is a grave issue. It can destroy people.

The Superboss will exercise extreme caution before any dismissal decision is made. He will ensure that all the proper warning procedures have been followed and that the person has had ample opportunity to improve. He will give him or her the chance to speak up and have his or her interests properly represented.

Above all the Superboss will be rigorous in ensuring that dismissal is fair and is handled in such a way that it preserves the person's dignity and minimizes loss of face. He'll be thoroughly compassionate in his approach, knowing that back home families will weep and children retreat into a silence of insecurity and incomprehensibility.

Dismissal brings hardship and agony, and what is more it is often unnecessary, if not unfair.

As a process of social rejection dismissal frequently destroys the last vestiges of inner confidence, dignity and pride a person might have.

The Superboss will try his utmost to avoid dismissal. But he will dismiss. He will dismiss those who thieve, who are violent, who abuse the company (and thus its people). He will dismiss those who continually fail to perform despite a thousand opportunities to improve. He will dismiss when there is no job to be done. But always, he will search for a way out, a way to avoid the dismissal. It might mean demotion, or transfer to another department. The Superboss knows that when the company hires people it makes a commitment to them. He will do his utmost to honor that commitment. Dismissal is a failure of that commitment, on both sides.

The Superboss will not tolerate hire-and-fire managers in his team, nor will he tolerate managers who do not confront potential dismissal situations.

Dismissal is a company failure, but regrettably failures sometimes occur.

ACTION TODAY

Make a mental note. Next time you are faced with a potential dismissal situation don't avoid the issue, but try to avoid the dismissal. Remind yourself that, whoever the person, he or she is a human being with a family and a face to maintain. So sit back, give the issue a little more time, think extremely carefully about it, consult your boss and your employee relations specialist. Then think again. But in the end you must decide. If the answer is dismissal, be scrupulous in handling it with dignity and compassion.

REMEMBER

For the SUPERBOSS, dismal is a last and sorrowful resort.

DISTANCE — TO MANAGE PEOPLE SUCCESSFULLY YOU HAVE TO WALK A TIGHTROPE BETWEEN BEING TOO CLOSE TO THEM AND TOO DISTANT.

Your best friend might live next door. You might go drinking at the same club together every Friday night. Your best friend might work in the same company as you.

How would you handle a situation where you were promoted to manage the department in which your best friend worked? What would you do if you discovered that his or her performance was so poor you had cause for dismissal? You cannot stop people being friends at work, in fact it is desirable. As a result of promotion you cannot stop them being friends because one is now the boss.

There can be no hard and fast rules. For the Superboss it's a matter of judgment with respect to each individual case. He draws a clear distinction between relationships at the workplace and relationships outside it. It could well be that he has two separate relationships with the same person. At the workplace, he will be wholly objective and maintain the appropriate distance. He will not pass on confidential information to his best friend, nor abuse social confidences his best friend gives to him.

Even so the Superboss will try to avoid close social relationships with the people who work for him, at the same time trying hard to develop close and effective working relationships. That's the tightrope between proximity and distance. If the Superboss is president of the company softball club he might drink beer with the team on Saturday night, but he'll separate that social relationship (albeit work-related) from the workplace relationships he has with certain members of the team. When it comes to management decisions he'll be totally objective and fair in dealing with a member of the softball team.

ACTION TODAY

Consider your relationship with every person who works in your company, division, department, or section. Can you honestly say that you treat each one equally, fairly, and objectively? Can you honestly say that you have not, in the last year or two, let a social relationship with an employee influence any decision you've made about that employee or others?

REMEMBER

The SUPERBOSS knows when to keep his distance and when to get closer.

EFFECTIVENESS

EFFECTIVENESS IS PUTTING WORDS INTO ACTION, AND ACTION INTO RESULTS.

The worst managers fail at stage one. They are all words and no action. The next worse are those who rush around, full of apparent action, but achieve little result.

You don't have to look far to see them; the committee managers, the memo-writing managers, the happy-chat managers — all full of words as usual. They achieve little and in ineffective companies don't get found out. Until the company goes down under.

The "flapper" is a person of too much action with too little time for it — forever on the phone, rushing from one meeting to the next, rearranging the appointment book. The "flapper" never really has time to fit you or anyone else in. He achieves little. His time will come, too.

The Superboss is effective, always thinking of how best to use his own and his people's time for achieving results. He is always evaluating priorities in his pursuit of profit and the right thing for his people. He knows it is more effective to spend half an hour with Linda Wallis discussing why she can't seem to get her transfer to External Affairs, rather than to attend the MRC committee to hear ten people waffle on about things they know little about!

The Superboss knows it is more effective to twist Personnel's arm to let him recruit a top-class engineer at a salary in the upper quartile, rather than accept their recommendation of a second-rate person at a lower salary.

The Superboss measures his effectiveness minute by minute, hour by hour, day by day. He is always asking himself, "What am I achieving by doing this, deciding that, planning for something else?" When he occasionally fails to achieve the desired result, he questions his own effectiveness. "Where did I go wrong? Why wasn't I effective?"

ACTION TODAY

Think carefully about every action you take today, the meetings you attend, the dictation you give, the decisions you make, the people you see. Question yourself rigorously, every half hour. What are all these words and actions achieving for the company, for profit and for people? Question yourself: "Am I being effective in every single thing I do? Am I achieving results?" If you kid yourself you're being totally effective then you have a lot to learn. There's always room for improvement, so find that room, sit down in it, and think, "How can I be more effective?" There must be an answer.

QUESTION

What makes a SUPERBOSS so effective?

EFFICIENCY ## IF YOU CAN'T MEASURE EFFICIENCY YOU MUST BE INEFFICIENT.

Profit is directly related to efficiency. The Superboss knows this and it never escapes his mind.

Efficiency is the ratio between the contribution made by an employee and the time, effort, and resource devoted to it.

Efficiency measures can be either quantitative or qualitative. The efficiency of a Production Manager can well be quantified, while that of a Welfare Officer will need a qualitative measure.

Sometimes one has to use more resource to be more efficient. For example, the Superboss may decide that the recruitment of three additional telephone operators to reduce average switchboard response time to five seconds might be more efficient than driving away potential customers who can't get through.

The Superboss has an eye for efficiency, not only of his staff but of himself. He will consider what is required of him personally to make the most profitable contribution to the business. He will have an eye on the key issues he should address, the problems he should attend to, the people he should see, the development activities he should pursue. In doing so he won't cram his appointment book full, knowing that the most efficient way of dealing with unexpected problems and issues is to schedule plenty of unallocated time.

ACTION TODAY

Go for a long walk, sit down on a park bench (if it's sunny) or in a cafe (if it's cold). Spend half an hour letting your mind run free and trying to identify three important efficiency improvements in the utilization of your own time at work. Make a mental note.

Walk back and take immediate action to implement these.

REMEMBER

The SUPERBOSS hasn't the time to be inefficient.

ENCOURAGEMENT — TO BE ENCOURAGED IS TO BE MOTIVATED.

Encouragement should always be genuine.

Be suspicious when that glum-faced manager who normally can't be bothered approaches with a sickly smile and says, "I was encouraged by the way you dealt with that Foxlee situation recently." (That was three months ago and this is the first time it's been mentioned to you.) "I wonder if you could help out over the weekend with an urgent problem at Draper's?"

Encouragement should be both genuine and frequent. You cannot just turn it on when you want something. That's a device; it's false and people won't believe you.

The Superboss is always encouraging his people. It's because he's genuinely encouraged himself. "At this rate of progress the order will be delivered two weeks ahead of schedule," he will tell them encouragingly. He'll call up a junior and say "I was really encouraged to learn about this great new idea of yours . . . ."

The Superboss will take the supervisor by the arm, walk him around, prop up the railing and look down at the assembly line. "It's going well, Bill," he'll say. "The line is running smoothly, your people seem very keen, the housekeeping is excellent, and what's more you've exceeded your targets each day this week. I'm encouraged, Bill; after last week's fiasco you've turned it right around."

To seek encouragement the Superboss is always looking for the positive things people are doing. He's desperate to encourage his people and puts himself out to do so for he knows that's the best way to motivate them.

And when things get rough he'll still encourage them, asking them to bear with him because he's got that much faith things will get better. And when the Superboss is around they normally do.

ACTION TODAY

Be encouraged and encourage. Go out of your way to find something that is going well and then encourage the people involved. If you happen to come across something that is going less well, don't frown, don't criticize, don't moan, don't throw up your hands in despair — but give a little encouragement. You've seen it all before, you know it will get better.

Give some genuine encouragement; it costs you nothing and is worth a lot.

QUESTION

Who encourages the SUPERBOSS?

ENERGY — WHO HAS THE ENERGY TO MANAGE PEOPLE SUCCESSFULLY?

This is not just a matter of taking the glucose tablets. Corpulent Frank Smith who leans back in his chair, puts his feet on the desk, puffs at his pipe, and gazes at the trees out of the window could take the tablets and it would make no difference. He could of course be thinking strategy, but it's unlikely. It's more likely that as Production Control Manager he lacks the energy for his job.

The Superboss is full of energy. It shows in his approach to work, in the things he gets done, in his excitement about new ideas, about progress. It shows in his enthusiasm for managing.

Not that he uselessly dissipates his energy by rushing around red-faced attempting to chase his tail. Energy in a Superboss leads to efficiency rather than useless activity. Instead of putting his feet up for half an hour, he'll pop down to the factory floor and see how things are going, or he'll make an impromptu telephone call to research and development for a progress report on the new product.

The energy of a Superboss gives him stamina, resilience, toughness, and the ability to accomplish a work program in half the time of a tired manager. To this extent the Superboss keeps fit, plays a sport if he can, walks, jogs, and ensures he doesn't put on too much weight. He'll eat light lunches and avoid alcohol during the day. He'll take pride in remaining healthy.

The Superboss always has the energy to see people. His energy shows; people know it and it energizes them too.

ACTION TODAY

Answer this question: How often do you daydream about retiring or getting some less frenetic, less demanding management position? If the answer is "frequently," then it is likely that you're lacking the energy for your job.

Now look on the positive side. Forget the drudgery and try to identify those things that you actually like about your management job. Jot them down. Now put some energy into those things. It might be something creative, or social, or administrative. Get up and get at it. Show you have some energy.

REMEMBER

Energy is one of the hallmarks of a SUPERBOSS.

ENTHUSIASM   ENTHUSIASM IS VISIBLE MOTIVATION.

Lack of enthusiasm shows. It shows on people's faces and in performance, or lack of it.

The Superboss is always enthusiastic about his team and what they can achieve. His enthusiasm shows, become infectious.

The Superboss knows that enthusiasm is a positive force, a demonstration of the motivation to achieve.

The Superboss avoids false enthusiasm, knowing that it will undermine his credibility and he will be branded a "con merchant."

His enthusiasm is always sincere and genuine. The Superboss is sincerely enthusiastic about the company (always stressing its good points, never playing on its weaknesses). He is genuinely enthusiastic about his people (knowing they can achieve so much). He is genuinely enthusiastic about the company's products and services (knowing they're the best). He's enthusiastic about his work, showing everyone around that he enjoys it, that it gives him a lot of satisfaction. He's enthusiastic about future challenges, about the prospect of overcoming problems.

His people love his enthusiasm; it makes them feel good, feel proud. It makes them enthusiastic in turn. The spirit of enthusiasm permeates the whole team.

But enthusiasm cannot be permanent. Occasionally the Superboss will feel low, dispirited. There will be a waning of his enthusiasm. His people will notice, will show concern. But they know how to lift him, make him enthusiastic again, for that's what he does with them when they're down and out.

ACTION TODAY

List everything about your work that you're enthusiastic about, examining in turn your company, your boss, your team, your colleagues, your company's products and services.

If you find you're enthusiastic about very little you have a serious problem. If you can't resolve it, then you must resign. You're no good to anyone if you're not enthusiastic about the company and your own contribution to it.

Now ask yourself whether your enthusiasm genuinely shows through. (You have to believe in something to be an enthusiast.) If you're not sure, it's because it doesn't show through, and this will be reflected in your team's lack of enthusiasm.

Starting today you must make sure you have some enthusiasm and also that it shows.

REMEMBER

The SUPERBOSS is a source of enthusiasm.

EXAMPLE A MANAGER CANNOT AVOID SETTING AN EXAMPLE.

If the example is to take two-and-a-half hours off for lunch and come back smelling of booze, then that's an example of how a manager values his or her time, an example of how he or she might expect others to behave.

If the example is to wear casual clothes to the office, then that's an example of the informal style the manager wants to establish.

If the example is to shout at people who are five minutes late, then that's an example of how the manager expects people to be treated.

Watch the Chief Executive. If he or she is polite, courteous, well-dressed, then that's an example of what is considered to be important in day-to-day behavior at the office. Others will follow.

The Superboss sets a good example. He always behaves in the way he expects his people to. If he expects his supervisors to participate in safety training courses for operational staff, then he'll set an example and participate himself from time to time. If he expects each of his managers to produce a monthly one-page progress report, then he'll do the same and distribute it to them. If he expects his people to stay late on a Friday evening, he'll set an example and stay late too.

But it will always be a good example. You will rarely hear a Superboss using offensive language or running down the company. Furthermore the Superboss will expect his people to set an example. He'll expect them to attend the awards ceremonies when managers in other divisions can't be bothered. He'll expect his managers to volunteer for operational duty when others won't.

The most important example, of course, is results. The Superboss wants to set an example to the company of what really can be achieved when you have a superb team.

ACTION TODAY

Be personal. Ask yourself what example you set your team. Whatever you do, however you behave, whatever you wear, whatever you say, whatever you achieve, whatever you decide, that will be the example. Is that the example you want others to follow? Or do you think you should rest on your laurels and let them set a different example? Determine for yourself what example you really want to set, then be determined in setting it.

QUESTION

Who sets the example for the SUPERBOSS?

EXPECTATIONS

EXPECTATIONS, LIKE MOUNTAINS, SHOULD BE HIGH AND VISIBLE.

If others don't know what to expect, nor what is expected of them, they will not only be at a loss but feel extremely insecure.

The Superboss expects a lot of his people. He expects them to work hard, to be committed, to help each other. He expects them to be honest. He expects them to do their best all the time. He expects them to make mistakes, but to learn from those mistakes and do better next time. He expects them to let him know about problems they can't resolve, which might impede progress. He expects them to air their grievances with him rather than let them fester. He expects them to be creative and come up with ideas for improvement.

The Superboss expects a great deal from others.

And his people expect a great deal from him.

They expect a Superboss to be fair and reasonable in all his dealings with them. They expect him to fight battles on their behalf, to consult them frequently, to communicate with them and let them know what's going on. They expect a Superboss to exercise his authority, expecting him to make clear-cut decisions. They expect him to take the lead in getting things done. They expect to see him from time to time; they expect him to get around and chat with them.

And when they talk to him they make their expectations clear, and he makes his clear to them.

ACTION TODAY

Set aside an hour in your appointment book (for today, tomorrow, or later, but it must be within the next two weeks) to spend with your immediate team to review expectations. Before you meet them prepare an "expectation list." There should be two columns:

1. What you expect of each of your team.
2. What you think they expect of you.

Keep the list short: each item should be no longer than one line.

When you meet the team get them to list what they think you expect of them. Then get them to list what they expect of you. If anyone asks, "What do you mean by an expectation?" answer, "I expect you to make your own interpretation."

Compare the various expectations. If there's a 90 percent overlap, you're probably a Superboss. If there's less, you've a lot to learn about them, and they about you.

REMEMBER
The SUPERBOSS expects no more the he is prepared to give.

EXPLANATION YOU CANNOT EXPLAIN AWAY BAD MANAGEMENT.

Explanation is the safeguard against arbitrariness. However, if you've made a bad decision, attempts to explain it away with invented reasons and excuses will severely undermine the credibility of management.

It happens frequently. A company will make a rushed decision at board level without thinking it through. The decision backfires on them. The board then seeks to find additional reasons to explain and justify their hasty decision.

An explanation that is invented after the decision is no explanation, but mere irrelevance. Nothing will reduce the credibility of management more.

The Superboss will only make a decision when he's confident of the reasons and therefore confident he can explain it to his people. It might be a zero pay increase, or a layoff of a group of people, or a decision to change the shift roster.

However, there are certain decisions for which the Superboss will refuse to give detailed explanations. While explaining that he selected the best person for the job, he will refuse to give more details as to why Wendy Morris got promoted and Jack O'Malley did not. He will refuse to explain why Peter Gorzel was dismissed yesterday. Confidential explanations will be reserved for the people immediately involved.

The discipline of providing sound explanations forces the Superboss to make consistently good decisions. It forces him to have the courage of his convictions. As a result he will be prepared to stand up in front of his people, or his boss, and account for that decision.

ACTION TODAY

Set yourself a new discipline. Before you make any decision affecting your people, your boss, or your company, shut your eyes and imagine yourself explaining that decision to them. If you are confident you can convince them, go ahead and make the decision.

If you are not confident you can explain, don't make the decision, and think again.

REMEMBER

The SUPERBOSS only makes a decision if he can produce a credible and genuine explanation.

 PEOPLE PROBLEMS ARE BEST RESOLVED FACE TO FACE.

Managers who attempt to resolve people problems by remote control normally fail. It's little use pinning on the notice board an instruction from the Operations Director about overtime control. The Superboss will call his people together and explain, face to face.

If the weekly overtime report shows that Baytree Section is still using excessive overtime the Superboss won't scribble a critical "What the hell's going on here?" annotation on the report and send it back to Mike Appleyard, the supervisor. He'll call him to the office and get him to explain face to face.

When Bob Keiller writes the Superboss a confidential memo saying he wants to discipline Liz Brodie, the Superboss will go to see Bob, face to face, and discuss the issue. He'll probably want to see Liz Brodie too, face to face, at some stage.

The Superboss knows that you cannot get to know people, nor they you, by writing memos or using the telephone. The Superboss therefore maximizes the opportunity for face-to-face contact, whether there's a problem or not. He wants to understand what people are all about. He wants to find out how genuine they are, what they're really made of, what they're really like.

The Superboss uses face to face contact for positive development reasons too. For example, if an excellent report comes his way from Paul West, a junior accountant, then he'll call Paul in for five minutes' face to face encouragement.

The Superboss encourages his people to face up to him too; that's why his door is always open, why he is never too busy to give time to people. The Superboss knows that effective employee relations are built on face to face contact and not by the remote application of hi-fi personnel policies and instructions from above.

The Superboss knows that face to face contact is a key to managing people successfully.

ACTION TODAY

Ask yourself how many new face to face contacts you have made during the last seven days. If the answer is zero, you're not a Superboss. Set yourself a target of making at least one new face to face contact with someone in your company each day.

REMEMBER

You don't know a SUPERBOSS unless you know him face to face.

FACING THE FACTS

THE WORST MANAGERS, WHICH IN MY WORST MOMENTS I THINK ARE THE MAJORITY, SUFFER FROM THE "OSTRICH SYNDROME."

Stick your head in the sand, but don't face the facts. Look the other way, duck, weave, and avoid the problem.

But not the Superboss; he faces the facts.

When Burt McManus makes a snide comment about the Chief Executive in front of the Superboss and his team, the Superboss doesn't pretend it's not a problem. He takes Burt aside after the meeting, speaks with him quietly and firmly and faces the facts. "What did you hope to achieve with your snide comment?" he asks. Burt McManus squirms and wriggles, but soon learns. Which he wouldn't have done if the Superboss had stuck his head in the sand.

When your Employee Relations specialist, your local staff representative, and a few others keep advising you that communications are poor in your department, don't go on the defensive and tell them that you brief your team once a month, as if the Employee Relations person and staff representative were idiots not to realize you were an expert in communication. Listen, learn, explore the problem with them, and face the facts. It might be you who is the problem. Then you'll learn. You'll have faced the facts. The way to become a Superboss.

There's that new secretary, Kate Honeywood. You're worried she's always ten minutes late, always chatting, takes hours to type a memo. You don't like to mention things to her for fear of damaging the relationship. Be nice to her and face the facts. "I could be wrong," you will tell her, "but I just feel uneasy about your time-keeping, your chatting, the time it takes to type a memo." She'll learn because you're a Superboss. A feeling is a fact. Face the facts. You could be wrong! You're a Superboss.

ACTION TODAY

This will be painful, so don't let anyone see. Go hide yourself away and search those uncomfortable corridors of your mind for things that really worry you at work, that you don't like to face.

Then face them, even if it means being honest for the first time with your boss, or someone in your team.

But first jot down your worries and analyze them carefully. Make sure you know what you're talking about. Then face up to the people who give you these worries and discuss the issues with them. You'll be surprised at the outcome. You'll feel better afterwards and your performance will improve dramatically.

QUESTION

Can your really face being a SUPERBOSS?

FAIRNESS — A MANAGER CAN BE RIGHT, A MANAGER CAN BE WRONG, BUT A MANAGER SHOULD NEVER BE UNFAIR.

Unfairness is a perception. It is a perception that you have recruited your old buddies from a previous company and unfairly discriminated against equally suitable people from within. It is a perception that the Chairman was able to afford a brand new Rolls Royce at the same time as clamping down on pay increases because of a decline in the business. It is a perception that you sacked Nick Baker because you had it in for him after the Peters' incident.

The perceptions can be, and often are, wrong. The Superboss goes to extreme limits to ensure that all his decisions are fair and furthermore are perceived to be so. He goes out of his way to ensure that personal prejudices (of which, like most human beings, he has many) never intrude upon his decision-making, never show up in conversation.

Furthermore, the Superboss will fight to the bitter end to ensure that his people are fairly treated. If Adele King's application for a transfer to Customer Relations is handled in an unfair and negligent manner, the Superboss will fight like mad to get her a fair hearing. If one of the company's expatriates has his home in Nigeria robbed and vandalized, the Superboss will go out of his way to ensure the expatriate is fairly treated. And if one of the company's Nigerian staff has his home robbed and vandalized the Superboss will go out of his way to ensure the Nigerian is fairly treated.

The way the Superboss treats John is the way he treats Mary, and the way he treats Mary is the way he treats Singh, Pamela, Umara, and everyone. His principles never vary in the way he behaves towards people. If it's fair to give written warnings for poor performance in the US, then it's fair to give written warnings in the UK, India, Mexico, and Ghana.

ACTION TODAY

This is an issue where perhaps you need the advice of the one closest to you. Go home this evening and discuss with your spouse (or partner or closest friend) whether or not they think you are perceived to be a fair boss. Tell them about the various personnel incidents you've handled over recent weeks. Tell your partner the truth about these incidents. Tell him or her about your doubts, your thoughts, your motives, the way you handled each incident.

As you spill the beans you might just realize (and your partner might just detect it) that on one or two occasions you've been less than fair. That will be a lesson.

REMEMBER

The SUPERBOSS prides himself on his fairness.

FEAR — YOU CANNOT AVOID FEAR AS A MOTIVATING FORCE, BUT YOU SHOULD NOT CAPITALIZE ON IT.

Management by fear has a certain Orwellian sound. Nobody should manage by fear. Having said that, fear of management will frequently exist.

Some will fear that a manager might be arbitrary, unfair, or downright callous in the decisions made about them. Others might fear the company will go out of business, that their jobs will be at risk. Liz Brodie might fear that because she doesn't have the right sort of chemistry with her boss, her salary and career progression might be pegged back. She might even fear she'll be fired.

The Superboss is sensitive to the fears of his people. Wherever possible he'll try to reassure them. What he will never do is exploit these fears. He will never threaten his people or, to put it bluntly, put the fear of God into them.

If there's a fear a key customer might switch to a competitor, the Superboss will acknowledge that fear and try to reassure his people that the company is doing its best to retrieve the situation. The Superboss is aware that fear is often based on ignorance, speculation, gossip, and prejudice. He tries to overcome this by giving his people the facts as best he can and as soon as he can.

If a Superboss senses there are personal fears among his people (for example, Eileen James fears Ed Cookson's fierce aggressive manner), he will try discreetly to remedy the situation, advising Eileen how to handle Ed, taking Ed aside and giving him some feedback about his behavior.

But certain fear will exist and should not be removed. The Superboss will tell his people, "Have no fear, if you don't perform I will take action." Employees should go in fear of breaking company rules, of abusing their colleagues, of not doing their best for the company.

ACTION TODAY

Take your Employee Relations specialist for a walk after lunch. (Buy him or her lunch first.) Ask what he or she thinks your people fear most at work. Push and probe and try to identify as many fears as possible. Then talk to one or two of your team about these fears. Modify the list as appropriate and separate them into "fears that can be addressed" and "fears that cannot be avoided."

Give priority to addressing the former. Your people will work more effectively for it.

REMEMBER

The only thing you should fear about a SUPERBOSS is his honesty and fairness in dealing with you.

| **FEEDBACK** | PERFORMANCE FEEDBACK IS ESSENTIAL TO PERFORMANCE IMPROVEMENT. WITHOUT IT, PERFORMANCE DETERIORATION IS INEVITABLE. |

I have yet to meet a single person who doesn't want to know how well he or she is doing. We all want reassurance that the contribution we're making is not only recognized but is the required one.

Without feedback people start making assumptions as to what is wanted of them, about standards, about how to behave. Without feedback team cohesion starts to dissolve and performance starts to deteriorate.

The Superboss gives feedback on a day-by-day basis, to his boss, his colleagues, his subordinates. Sometimes it's feedback on what he's been doing: this morning's negotiations, his visit to Microsoft yesterday, his meeting with Al Tusler at lunchtime.

At other times it's feedback about individual performance: "I thought that was a good report, Diana, although it would be helpful to have a summary to begin with." He'll take George Neal by the elbow, "I know you work hard, George, but let me give you some feedback. If you treat customers in the same abrupt aggressive way you treat your teammates then we've got a big problem looming up."

He'll see Susan Gonzales and tell her, "I thought you did an excellent job helping Stan out with that problem he had yesterday. He gave me some good feedback about you. . . ."

The Superboss knows that without constant feedback he cannot reinforce what he values as important for the team. No feedback means that nothing the team is doing is important and that the boss has more important things to do.

ACTION TODAY

Walk around your company and give some informal feedback to at least five people, whether or not they report directly to you. Try to be as positive as possible, looking for the good things they are doing. But don't avoid the negatives. Your people will appreciate your help if your feedback about "negatives" is made in a positive constructive helpful manner.

QUESTION

Who gives feedback to the SUPERBOSS?

FIGHTING

FIGHT FOR YOUR PEOPLE, FIGHT FOR YOUR PRINCIPLES, FIGHT FOR YOUR COMPANY, BUT DON'T FIGHT AMONG YOURSELVES.

You only have to put your ear to the ground in most organizations to hear the fighting.

When a team starts fighting among itself the results can be disastrous, albeit excellent for the people you're supposed to be fighting — your competitors in the marketplace. Internal fighting dissipates energy, is inefficient, saps morale, and is a reflection of extremely poor leadership.

The Superboss will not allow members of his team to fight each other. He'll bring them together, if necessary bang their heads together, but in any event he'll get them working together as opposed to working against each other.

The Superboss will fight battles, however. He'll fight to ensure his people receive a fair pay raise this year. He'll fight to ensure they have adequate tooling and working conditions. He'll fight to obtain a sensible allocation of budget for training his people. In fighting for his people the Superboss won't give up at the first round. He'll fight to the bitter end if he believes he's right and it's for the rights of his people.

Often the battle will be one of principle. If his people are being unfairly discriminated against in the allocation of office space he'll fight on the principle of fairness and equity. If they are being unfairly discriminated against in the battle for promotion because of the bad reputation of his predecessor, then he'll fight against prejudicial selection.

Although the Superboss will fight on the issues of rights, he knows he is not always right. He knows when to accept authority and when to challenge it. The Superboss is far from being an extremist or a militant.

ACTION TODAY

Clean the whiteboard, or erect a flipchart. Take a black pen and draw a diagram of the battlelines in (a) your company, (b) your area. List the protagonists (be careful) and the main warring factions. It might be, for example, Quality Control versus Production, or Finance versus Personnel.

Display the diagrams in your office. Do nothing until someone comes in and comments. Use this opportunity to start a peace initiative.

REMEMBER

Whatever the fight, the SUPERBOSS fights for the company and its people.

FIRMNESS — TO BE FIRM IS TO KNOW WHEN TO STOP LISTENING AND WHEN TO INSIST.

The problem with many managers is that they stake out a position too early. They make promises they cannot fulfill. They issue threats which everyone knows cannot be carried out. When pressure is put on that position they cannot hold firm, they have to bend.

Other managers ignore problems, or accept explanations too readily. They accept excuses and do not attempt to get at the root causes of problems. These are managers who do not hold firm on certain key principles of management. They allow people to pull the wool over their eyes, or to cover up. They even turn a blind eye when standards loosen, when people start abusing the company, stealing, taking longer break periods, coming in late.

The Superboss has certain principles on which he will always hold firm and his people know it. Within this framework of principle he will give others plenty of scope to do their own thing.

The Superboss will never stake out a position too early only to retract it later. He would not, for example, insist on reducing the manning level on a machine only to find later it was wholly impracticable, as his staff had been telling him all along.

The Superboss only makes a decision if he knows he can hold firm on it. If he suspects that he might have to bend on a potential decision, he won't make it. He would not, for example, issue a disciplinary warning if he had any doubt that it might not hold firm on appeal.

Being firm means being sure. It means that you are confident and that others will be confident in you. If you don't hold firm, people won't know where they stand and will push you all over the place.

Occasionally the Superboss will make a mistake and not be able to hold firm on a decision. He'll then admit his mistake and change the decision.

ACTION TODAY

Make a critical review of some of the key decisions you've made over recent months. Have you had to retract on any? If yes, ask yourself, "Why didn't I hold firm? Did I admit my mistake? If there were additional factors arising after I made the decision, why didn't I take them into account before I made the decision?" Discipline yourself never to make a decision unless you are completely confident it will hold firm.

REMEMBER

The SUPERBOSS is always fair and consistent.

FLAIR — MANAGING PEOPLE SUCCESSFULLY REQUIRES FLAIR, A CERTAIN *JE NE SAIS QUOI*.

Flair is all to do with the unexpected.

Dull managers are so predictable, so unimaginative. You know exactly what they're going to do, and what they're going to do is be unexciting, monotonous, mundane, boring, and frequently negative.

The Superboss can be predictable too. He's predictably reliable, predictably firm, fair, and consistent. You can predict that he's going to do his very best for the company and its people.

But within that framework of predictability the Superboss will demonstrate a high degree of flair for managing people successfully. The Superboss has a flair for getting you on his side. For example, he'll take you into his confidence when you least expect it. He'll give you support when you thought he had more important matters on his mind. He'll come and seek your advice when you expected him to go elsewhere. The Superboss has a flair for making your work exciting, interesting, a flair for making you feel good about what you do, a flair for making you feel important.

The Superboss also has a flair for getting to the heart of a problem. Whether it's his instinct or his greater experience, he always seems to arrive at the unexpected solution when everyone else has given up. He has a flair for overcoming obstacles and seeing his way through to the end. His team might be despairing as to how they can achieve further cost reductions, but the Superboss has the flair for finding that little pot of gold (unused stock) which has been overlooked.

And how does the Superboss develop flair? There's no single answer. He has a nose for a problem, an eye for a detail, an ear for the other person. He has tasted success and has a touch of class. By developing his senses he has developed an instinct for getting people on his side, for overcoming problems, and for reaching the winning post first. His flair will probably derive from a distillation of his experience, knowledge, skills, and his enthusiasm and awareness of what's going on.

ACTION TODAY
Think of one person in your company, whether or not he or she reports to you, who in your opinion demonstrates flair. Carefully observe and study that person from a distance. Try to analyze why that person has flair. Try to learn from his or her approach to work.

REMEMBER
Show your SUPERBOSS you have flair. It might be the last thing he expects of you.

FOLLOW THROUGH

FOLLOW THROUGH AND YOUR PEOPLE WILL FOLLOW TOO.

It happens when you follow through. It happens to be what you said you'd do.

Many don't. Bob Lewis said he'd send you a copy of the Stage 3 report, and didn't. Barbara O'Donnell said she'd phone back to confirm that booking, and didn't. Gary Cordello said he'd drop by with the proofs, and didn't.

They didn't follow through, but the Superboss will. He'll allow them a little latitude, then he'll phone Bob, Barbara, and Gary. The Superboss knows that if he doesn't follow through, nobody will. He sets the example and his people follow, because if they don't he'll be following through and asking why.

But it's more than that. When Frank Michnik mentions that he's going into the hospital next week, the Superboss follows through, finds out how he is, sends some magazines and a card, pops in to see him when he returns.

When Gloria Gales says that Personnel seems to be procrastinating over the recruitment of a new clerk, the Superboss follows through. He'll ring Gloria in two days time and ask how she is progressing with the recruitment, and if she's still getting hassled he'll follow through with a phone call to Personnel on her behalf.

And when the Superboss promises Adrian Surtees some training in Finance for non-financial people he'll follow through and make sure he gets it.

ACTION TODAY

Call in your secretary and do a systematic check through your appointment book for the last few weeks. Try to recall what happened at each meeting you attended. Try to remember if you promised to follow through on anything, and whether you actually did. Check your recent mail the same way. Follow through immediately if you've forgotten to do so.

ACTION TOMORROW

Cast your mind back over recent informal encounters with your people. Is there anything they mentioned to you which perhaps you should now follow through?

ACTION NEXT WEEK

If you feel you're particularly weak in follow-through techniques, devise some sort of note-taking and checking system, and rigorously use it.

REMEMBER

Always assume the SUPERBOSS will follow through.

GESTURES — A GESTURE IS A BENEVOLENT MOVE TOWARDS YOUR PEOPLE.

Gestures can have a very positive impact. A gesture can be sending a card to someone who is sick, a thank-you note to someone who has rendered particularly good service to the company.

A gesture is a wink to someone who knows, a light slap on the back as a measure of appreciation (but take care to avoid any hint of sexual harassment). A gesture is an extra day off for someone who voluntarily worked late without overtime.

The Superboss makes genuine gestures. They are unexpected but positive behaviors, never predictable and never taken as a right. They tend to be small but magnanimous movements in another person's direction. Gestures are made without request, without negotiation and without trial. Gestures are a token of trust, a demonstration that the Superboss is prepared to "give a little" without asking.

Gestures give the Superboss power. They cost little in time or resource but are of immense value in motivating people. But they have to be positive and they have to be genuine.

As a gesture of appreciation the Superboss will take his team for a Chinese meal after a hard time at work. As a gesture of welcome he'll pen a personal note at the foot of the transfer offer to Anu Patel. As a congratulatory gesture he'll send Diana Kendal a bottle of champagne when she passes her accountancy examinations second time round. As a gesture of concern he'll phone Leo Hammond at home when he's laid up on his back, and ask if there's anything he wants done.

ACTION TODAY

Make a gesture today. A positive gesture. Buy your secretary a box of chocolates. (I'm sure she's great — you wouldn't be a Superboss if she was otherwise.) Send a handwritten thank-you note to the engineer who worked to midnight to get the new multitracking system working again.

QUESTION

Can you make a gesture to show you are a SUPERBOSS?

GIVING TIME — A MANAGER'S HIGHEST PRIORITY IS TO GIVE TIME TO HIS PEOPLE.

The worst managers are those you cannot get in to see, whose secretaries are haughty obstructionists to say the least.

The worst managers are those who give little time to their staff; who are always in meetings with the President, or visiting Saudi Arabia, San Francisco, or Singapore, or writing speeches, or dealing with some urgent problem down at C Plant. They are managers who would rather be studying reports on new product evaluations than seeing people; who would rather be having expensive three-hour lunches with customers than appraising people.

The Superboss has an absolute rule. Unless he is on vacation or away from base and uncontactable, he will give time to any of his people within 24 hours of their asking for it. No matter how busy he is, no matter how crammed his appointment book, if Maria Aziz wants five minutes of his time, he will, without question, find her five minutes of his time within 24 hours. It might have to be at eight in the morning, or six in the evening, but he'll go out of his way to give her the time.

But the Superboss doesn't wait to be asked. He finds time for getting around so that people can raise any issue they like as he passes by.

For the Superboss giving time to his people is the most important thing he can do. It is his people who deliver the results, who have the problems, who need his help. He'll therefore give time to all aspects of managing people, to their selection, to their training and development, to their motivation, to solving their problems, to communications, and to their welfare.

He'll give time as well, of course, to his boss and his colleagues. He finds the time by not over-committing his appointment book, by not attending unnecessary time-consuming committee meetings and, I'm afraid, by not working strict 9 to 5 hours.

ACTION TODAY

Look back over your appointment book for the last four weeks. Calculate how much time you have genuinely given to your people. At least 80 percent should be on people issues, and at least 40 percent should be made freely available to them one way or another to raise any issues and problems. Should you be nowhere near 80 percent "people time" and 40 percent "availability time," then more than likely you will have serious people problems in your area.

QUESTION

Would you give time to a SUPERBOSS?

GLORY THE GLORIES OF MANAGEMENT ARE NEVER VISIBLE.

Anyone who owns up to being a Superboss is not a Superboss. He or she is a glory-seeking surface manager. No Superboss will ever admit to being one.

A Superboss doesn't seek glory. He has sufficient faith that his time will come for promotion, for salary increases, and that in due course those who make such decisions will recognize his super contribution. If such decisions don't come his way, if he's passed over for promotion, or doesn't get the salary increase he thinks he deserves, then he'll try to understand why, try to learn a little, try to do better next time. And if he concludes it's a bad decision, he'll put it down to Fate. Everybody makes bad decisions from time to time.

The Superboss is more interested in the glory of his team, identifying their successes, and giving them credit. He never takes credit himself. He goes out of his way to recognize outstanding performance by members of his team and is wholly objective in doing so. The Superboss always avoids the "blue-eyed boy" syndrome.

When the Chief Executive comes to address the department and congratulate them on their fine performance last month, the Superboss in reply says it was all due to his team.

The Superboss knows that glory is something that is given, not taken. He is not impressed by those who keep telling him they are doing a fantastic job. He'll take them aside: "Don't you trust me? Why do you keep telling me you're doing a great job? Isn't it my job to know? When you're doing a great job, I'll tell you." And the Superboss will.

ACTION TODAY

Make your team feel proud, give them some glory. If you can't, what are you doing? Aren't they any good? Get them featured in the company newspaper, or draft a letter for the Chief Executive to sign thanking them for having pulled out all stops to get that export order out. Or when Jane Smith comes in on Monday to tell you she's completed the London marathon in record time (for her), call the team together, congratulate her. Give Jane Smith some glory, she deserves it.

REMEMBER

The SUPERBOSS knows that those who seek glory never achieve it.

NOT TO HAVE A GRIEVANCE PROCEDURE IS A FAILURE ON THE PART OF MANAGEMENT. TO USE A GRIEVANCE PROCEDURE IS ALSO A FAILURE ON THE PART OF MANAGEMENT.

The grievance procedure must be there as a safety valve. But it should be used rarely.

The Superboss creates an atmosphere in his department where people feel free to air grievances. He doesn't make them feel threatened, or guilty, or silly if they raise a grievance. If someone raises a grievance with him, the Superboss will give it his highest priority. He'll create time within 48 hours to look at the problem and try to get it resolved. He'll draw in other people and then refer back to the person with the grievance as soon as possible.

If the grievance is outside his own jurisdiction, for example, about lack of car-parking spaces for disabled people, or about the office always being locked on a Saturday when an employee wants to work voluntarily, then the Superboss will pursue the grievance on behalf of the employee, taking it up with the appropriate person. The last thing the Superboss will say is "I can't sort out car parking, that's not my responsibility." Nor will he say, "if you're silly enough to want to work on Saturday you will have to work at home."

The use of the formal grievance procedure in an organization is, in the Superboss's eyes, failure of the supervisor or manager to whom the grievance was first addressed. The immediate manager should be accountable for progressing and resolving any grievance before they get into formal procedure.

ACTION TODAY

Go and have an informal drink with your immediate reportees at lunchtime or after work. Ask if they can recall the last time a grievance was raised in their area. Mention that you'd like to be aware of any grievances their people have. The last thing you want to happen is walk around and be caught with a grievance the immediate manager hasn't reported to you.

QUESTION

Can you imagine having a grievance against a SUPERBOSS?

HANDLING PEOPLE EVERY EMPLOYEE IS UNIQUE AND NEEDS TO BE HANDLED IN A UNIQUE WAY.

The Superboss recognizes the uniqueness of each individual who works in his area. He recognizes that Andy Newton is an aggressive machine-minder with only two interests in life, women and football. The Superboss therefore handles him with a combination of firmness and humor, tolerating only so much talk about women.

The Superboss recognizes that Felix Fry is a smiling hypocritical chameleon and he has to watch what he says to him and handle him in a discreet way. The Superboss recognizes that Liza Meszaros is the fastest word-processor operator in the company, but is liable to get upset with the most minor unintended provocation. He will handle her with kid gloves and tend to praise her efficiency frequently.

The Superboss makes no gross assumptions about his people. He doesn't assume they'll all behave the same way, and have the same interests as he does. If next year's budget is the biggest thing on his mind, he doesn't assume it will be the biggest thing on theirs.

To handle each employee effectively the Superboss must be sensitive to their needs and their interests. He tries hard to learn about them, their personalities, their skills and attributes, and he modifies his behavior accordingly, joking more with Ian Butcher and being more sympathetic to Felicity O'Hagan. He will give Anna Romanov all the time she needs because she asks for little, but he will always have to be diplomatic and cut short Patrick Dessan when he waffles on too much.

The Superboss knows that with skillful and genuine handling each person will perform more effectively, appreciating his sensitivity and knowing he's not treating them all like performing dogs.

ACTION TODAY

Think about your immediate team. Jot down the key differences in their personalities, and then the different ways in which you handle them. Consider whether you could handle each person more effectively. If Lynda Joel is shy and retiring are you really sensitive towards her? Or do you just not bother with her, ignore her because she says little? Perhaps there is a better way.

REMEMBER

People will always know how to handle a SUPERBOSS.

HONESTY NOBODY EVER DISPUTES IT IS DISHONEST TO PAD YOUR EXPENSES, PUT YOUR HAND IN THE TILL, OR TELL LIES ON YOUR CAREER RESUME. BUT DISHONESTY IS MORE SUBTLE THAN SIMPLE FRAUD AND BLATANT UNTRUTH.

Dishonesty in management is more widespread on the subject of the declaration of motives and the statement of opinions. It is often prevalent through the omission of certain facts and a gloss on the balance.

To mislead by omission is to be dishonest. Dishonesty in management is far-reaching because companies assume that business confidence will be lost if the naked truth (more losses, more disputes, more complaints) is told. This creates a climate of dishonesty and distrust throughout the organization and beyond. One dishonest statement will lead to a thousand dishonest statements. No one will trust anything the company says.

Dishonesty among managers is present in companies stricken with politics. For example, the scheming manager who paints a very black picture of what is going on in another department when talking to the Chief Executive is being dishonest in failing to declare his motives: an interest in managing that other department. The manager who tells the boss everything is going well when the problems are countless is similarly dishonest. There are countless other examples: the manager who tells his staff he is looking into the catering problem when in fact he's forgotten all about it; the Financial Director who shuffles millions into hidden accounts to avoid the books looking too good before an audit.

No person can be a Superboss by being dishonest in any shape or form, whether it be by misleading statements or blatant omission of the facts.

ACTION TODAY

Don't turn away from this page. Confess all now! To yourself. Whether it's politically inexpedient or not, ruthlessly purge yourself of every single dishonesty, every single distortion, every single misleading statement and omission you've made over recent months.

Then make a vow always to be honest. Honesty pays, even if you have to lose your job in the process. A clean conscience and no job pays greater dividends than distortion and dishonesty at work.

REMEMBER

The SUPERBOSS is honest not only with others around him, but with himself.

HUMILITY | HUMILITY FOR A MANAGER IS A POSITIVE STRENGTH.

The manager who knows it all has no humility. The manager who gives little time to others has no humility.

The manager who doesn't listen has no humility. The manager who never admits a mistake has no humility. The manager who is not interested in people's problems has no humility. There are many such managers. They are merciless in the pursuit of their own selfish ambitions. They will push others aside, ignore them, neglect them, even destroy them in their merciless mission to get to the top.

They don't realize that their people want to go places too.

The Superboss will have the humility to respect this. He will have the humility to learn from them because he has the humility to acknowledge he doesn't have all the answers. He has the humility to accept that Ray Cotton can do a far better job supervising engineers than he ever could. Why should the Superboss even attempt to tell Ray Cotton how to do his job? That would be a total lack of humility.

The Superboss gains strength, credibility, and respect because he has sufficient humility to learn from the Ray Cottons of this world, to accept their advice and help. In return the Superboss will go out of his way to help Ray Cotton.

Humility is the process of recognizing your own several weaknesses and respecting other people's substantial strengths.

ACTION TODAY
When you sit in the bath tonight, think about your own weaknesses in relation to your management task, and then the strengths of those in your team.

ACTION TOMORROW

Take one personal weakness, show some humility, and ask the person in your team who has the corresponding strength to give you some advice and help you.

REMEMBER

The SUPERBOSS has sufficient humility to know that he has as many weaknesses as his people have strengths.

INCENTIVES · INDIVIDUAL INCENTIVES ARE INCOMPATIBLE WITH TEAM SPIRIT.

The carrot-and-stick theory went out of fashion a long time ago. We'll dwell on carrots here.

If the company offered you an extra week's salary for doubling your output tomorrow how would you react? Unless you're a lazy bastard (and why reward lazy bastards?) you would rightly reply that you're already working at maximum output. Furthermore, you receive a fair level of pay, which reflects your contribution.

However, if the company offered you a similar incentive for selling twice as much tomorrow, how would you react?

The fact that sales people eat carrots and few others do creates enormous problems and inequities. What is the incentive for the person who masterminds the advertising, who organizes sales-support services, who provides back-up customer services, who distributes the product, who designs the packaging?

These days, unless you're self-employed, you cannot work as a one-man band. Even sales people out on the road need a back-up team.

If there's to be any incentive the Superboss believes it should be a team incentive. With the exception of a company profit-share incentive (available to all employees) the Superboss would prefer any team incentive to be non-financial. Occasionally he might say, "Look guys, we've got an urgent job on this week, an extra ten tons for Dennett's. If we can get it out on time by Friday close of day, there's a bottle of whiskey in it for each of you." Or he might say to his sales team, "If we can win that contract with Billson's, we'll have a night out on the town."

ACTION TODAY

Do a little gentle thinking. Think about yourself. Is there any incentive the company could offer you which would motivate you to improve your performance? If the answer is "yes," consult your boss about your performance improvement—the answer probably lies in his or her hands.

Now think about your people. Is there any incentive you could offer them which would motivate them to improve their performance?

Is the answer any different from your first answer? If you say "yes," you have a problem. You cannot allow incentives to be a substitute for your own management incapability.

REMEMBER

To be recognized as a SUPERBOSS is incentive enough.

INITIATIVE — TAKING THE INITIATIVE IS THE FIRST STEP TO SUCCESS.

In a complex competitive world the opportunities for success are everywhere, but often difficult to see. It takes initiative to spot them, seize them, and exploit them.

The Superboss is full of initiative. He sees opportunities everywhere — opportunities for his people, for his company, for profit, for improvement. He takes the initiative and seizes them. For example, an employee might mention in passing that he has an idea for improving the stock control procedure. The Superboss will take the initiative and pursue the idea on the employee's behalf. For example, his people might be having persistent problems with quality control. The Superboss will take the initiative, have a look, call in an outside expert, and try to get the problem solved.

The Superboss might see the opportunity for developing a new market in the North. He'll take the initiative to step onto an airplane and size up the opportunity himself, developing his contacts in the process.

The Superboss also encourages initiative among his employees. He'll encourage initiatives to improve performance, to improve relationships, to resolve problems, and to come up with new ideas. Should his people want to experiment with new maintenance schedules, he'll let them take the initiative. If they want to take the employee representatives away for a weekend seminar on employee relations, he'll let them take the initiative.

The Superboss will never stand in the way of initiative.

ACTION TODAY

Take one initiative today (i.e., something you hadn't thought of yesterday) to manage your people more successfully.

ACTION NEXT WEEK

Identify what initiatives each member of your team has taken over the last three months.

ACTION NEXT MONTH

Review "initiative" with your team.

REMEMBER

It takes initiative to become a SUPERBOSS.

INSPIRATION IT TAKES INSPIRATION TO GET OUT OF THE RUT AND BEAT THE COMPETITION.

There are greater experts on lateral thinking than me. But I've seen the disastrous results vertical thinking achieves. The well-ploughed furrows of attempting to crack a constantly recurring problem, the repetitive exhortations to improve efficiency, cut down costs and work harder.

I've seen the despair when the competition steals a lead in the marketplace with a new product; the despair when the unions once again respond threateningly and aggressively to the familiar pleas for pay restraint.

Companies, managers, and people get trapped into ruts from which they seem unable to extricate themselves. But one doesn't have to look far for the inspiration to get out of these ruts. There are always people in the organization who will find the lateral solution.

The Superboss seeks inspiration through his people. He won't hack away at well-tried but demonstrably unsuccessful solutions. He'll be stimulating, inspiring his people to be creative, to think laterally, to come up with new ideas, new approaches. He'll give them plenty of scope. He'll create a climate which can achieve inspired results.

For the Superboss inspiration is second nature; he's always searching for it and frequently finds it.

ACTION TODAY

What inspires you?

Who inspires you?

When are you inspired?

Why are you inspired?

If you're never inspired, have an inspired guess at the answers to these questions.

Starting today, create among your people a climate of inspiration. Sit them down if necessary, spell out the biggest problem facing the department and ask for inspired ideas on how to solve that problem. Rank the ideas and shortlist three. Now ask your team to evaluate each shortlisted idea. There is one condition. The implementation of the idea must be the responsibility of an individual or group of individuals within the team. They must be prepared to commit to that responsibility. If you need help to discover some inspired ideas call in a consultant or your personnel person.

REMEMBER

You'll never find a SUPERBOSS lacking in inspiration.

INTEGRITY — WHAT PRICE INTEGRITY WHEN THE FITTEST MUST SURVIVE AND THE KILLER INSTINCT PREVAILS? IN OTHER WORDS, CAN YOU GET TO THE TOP AND STILL HAVE INTEGRITY?

There is a language among managers—"back-stabbing," "dropping someone in the mire," "covering one's tracks," "turning into a bootlicker," "running with the hare and hunting with the hounds," "becoming a sacrificial lamb," "entering the rat race," or "being out for blood."

It is the language of the jungle. It is the language of frightened people who manage in the dark, beneath the surface of honesty, respectability, and principle. It is the language of an organization lacking in integrity. It is the language where fairness and justice is seen not to prevail.

In the jungle the rules are never clear. You have to make them up as you go along in order to survive. You have to be on the "right" side of Tom Mercer from Finance, or be "in with" Bessie Vincent in Employee Relations. You should never "cross swords" with the Chairman, otherwise he'll be out "gunning for you" (to mix metaphors) .

The Superboss stands aside from the jungle. He exudes integrity. Everyone will know that he is a man of principle, is 100 percent honest. You will never find the Superboss playing games with his people's livelihoods.

The Superboss will refuse to join in any form of jungle fighting, even if it means putting his job on the line. The Superboss will always seek to make, and obtain, fair and objective decisions. The rules by which he manages will always be clear to the people in his organization. The Superboss will have no select band of "blue-eyed boys" or mercenary "jungle fighters." You will never find the Superboss going for someone's throat or trying to creep in through "the back door."

The Superboss doesn't spy on his people, nor does he try to catch them out. The Superboss doesn't go on witch hunts, nor does he look for scapegoats.

The Superboss knows that profit is best achieved when employees and customers alike respect a company for its integrity. That integrity will be reflected in its management and leadership.

ACTION TODAY

Do you pride yourself on your integrity? If not, why not? Look at the managers in your company, those who work for you, those who are your bosses, those elsewhere. How many visibly demonstrate a high degree of integrity? Put yourself at the top of the list and lead the way.

REMEMBER

The integrity of a SUPERBOSS should be beyond questions.

INTEREST — TO PROFIT THROUGH PEOPLE YOU MUST BE INTERESTED IN PEOPLE.

People can be quite difficult and you can lose interest in them rapidly. Some managers are much more interested in machines, financial figures, production plans, developing new products, or attending sales conferences overseas. Some managers are not at all interested in their people. Some managers will devote more than 80 percent of their time to these non-people-oriented activities.

If you are not interested in your people, genuinely interested, then I can guarantee they won't be interested in you and the company.

The Superboss shows interest in his people. He often asks how they're getting along. He'll approach Ossie Brett, the green-haired punk, and say, "I bet you had a good time raving it up at Blaze's Saturday night." He'll get Ossie to talk about his interests, about Blaze's, the heavy-metal rock, the leather, the beer. For Kevin Hughes it might be football, for Marilyn Fields it might be the Italian meal she had with her boyfriend.

And the Superboss will take an interest in what's happening on the production line. "How are you finding this new high-speed drill?" he'll ask Bernie Britz. "Don't you find it a bit chilly in here?" he'll ask Zelda Wade — and then do something about it.

To take an interest in his people the Superboss will spend more than 80 percent of his time on people-related activities, walking through the department, chatting with people, reviewing progress, taking an interest in their training, in their careers, in their working conditions, in their problems, in everything that has an impact on their effectiveness and satisfaction at work.

He knows that interest is a two-way street. If he's interested in them, and shows it, more than likely they will reciprocate.

ACTION TODAY

Get off your behind and take a walk around your department. Take an interest in what your people are doing; casually chat with them about how things are. Don't pry into their private lives, but do take an interest in their families, in their social lives, in their sport.

Discipline yourself to get out and about, taking an interest, at least four times a week. Get other people interested, too, in what's going on in your area. Invite the Personnel Manager to walk around with you, or the Divisional Director, or Chief Executive.

You'll be surprised how people respond to interest.

QUESTION

Who takes interest in the SUPERBOSS?

INVOLVEMENT THE MORE YOU INVOLVE THE LESS LIKELY THE REVOLT.

Involvement concerns cohesion and contribution. Lack of involvement will lead to divisiveness and retribution. Involvement is the process of securing commitment. If you are involved, you will contribute and you will commit. If you are involved, you will identify with the team's goals; you will want to share in the success.

Involvement requires time, and the Superboss takes time to involve his people. It requires a tremendous effort because other people can be so frustrating at times. They can appear to slow you down and you will want to ignore them and not involve them. But nowadays people will revolt if you don't involve them. You might not see the rebellion to begin with; it might fester under the surface for a long time. But in the end, if you don't involve them they will revolt and you won't be there. They will.

The Superboss involves his people in whatever he can, mostly in matters concerning them directly, whether it be a new factory layout, the purchase of a new type of truck, or methods of improving efficiency. In involving others he doesn't abdicate his responsibilities. They know and he knows that the final decision will always be his. He will have to take responsibility for it. By involving his people the decision is more likely to be right. By involving his people he secures their commitment to the implementation of that decision. Instead of resisting the introduction of new technology they will demand it, if they've been involved in the evaluation studies.

The Superboss not only involves his people in the company's problems, he gets involved in their problems. He encourages them to bring their problems to him. He involves himself in trying to sort them out, in trying to help.

ACTION TODAY

Write down the three most important projects you have at the moment. Against each project list the names of those involved. Now list the people, or the groups of people who will be affected by that project.

Is a representative cross-section of people from this latter list involved in each project?

If the answer is no, involve them today before it's too late.

REMEMBER

You cannot be a member of the SUPERBOSS's team without being involved.

 **THE MANAGER WHO JOINS IN IS NEVER LEFT BEHIND.**

How can you understand if you don't join in? How can you appreciate the problem of emptying sludge tanks if you've never emptied them yourself? If you have, you might be a little more sympathetic to a request for improved protective gear.

The Superboss joins in not only because he wants to help, but because he wants to understand. Nobody expects a Superboss to type, or program computer systems, but they do expect him to join in and load pallets when they're short of staff and there's an urgent job; they do expect him to pick up a ringing telephone and answer when the whole office is rushed off its feet; they do expect him to serve in the shop when they're one short at the counter for a while.

There can be no set pattern to joining in. Some Superbosses might pop down at the end of every shift to help clear up so everyone can get away on time. Others might join in when there's a rush order to be dispatched. Others might join in on a regular basis because they want to understand what's going on in the factory. Others automatically join in to help their staff resolve a serious problem. Others just join in for the sheer fun of it.

In joining in nobody expects the Superboss to do more than he's capable of.

The Superboss does not let union demarcation lines prevent him from joining in. He'll explain, he'll discuss it with the union, but he'll insist he must join in. It's not to take his people's jobs away from them, far from it. It's to help understand their jobs; it's to help his people. It will make them feel important because the Superboss will never be able to do as good a job as them.

ACTION TODAY

Wander around your department and just join in; help push that trolley they're struggling with, pick up a bin and empty it when you're chatting to the cleaners, "I hope you don't mind me helping." Lick a few envelopes in the mail room. Ask the training manager whether you can join in his next management course. Sit with the transport drivers. Take a van out with one of them and perhaps drive it for a few miles to give the driver a rest. Join in wherever you can today! They'll respect you for it.

REMEMBER
The SUPERBOSS joins because he want to help and he wants to understand.

JUDGMENT

MANAGEMENT PREJUDICE IS THE BIGGEST THREAT TO FAIR AND OBJECTIVE JUDGMENT.

Prejudice within management is a disease. I am not talking only about racial, religious, or sexual prejudice. I am talking about the way managers make prejudicial decisions about people.

Managers allow many things to cloud their judgment. It might be the primary colored shirts Roland Cribbs wears, or Frank Harper's unfortunate obesity. It might be that Eddie Romain has a clipped staccato-like accent, or that Angie Solloway breeds dogs in her spare time. Often it's more subtle than that. "There were problems with Sylvan Shaloma a few years ago." One is not sure what the problems were, but one is left with a doubt.

Managers allow emotions to affect their judgment, or opinions passed on by other people. Someone will say: "I wouldn't even consider Jason Kenny for that post; he's useless." Jason Kenny is ruled out before a fair and objective judgment can be made about him.

Prejudice comes in all shapes and colors. There can be prejudice against unions ("They're all communists or Mafiosi"); or against people from Personnel ("A lot of useless do-gooders"); or against people from the Maudelonde Factory down the road ("They're a bunch of lazy bastards").

Prejudice at best is based on half-baked half-truths, and at worst on blind assumptions and total ignorance. Prejudice often occurs because people don't belong to the "clan."

The Superboss tries hard to eliminate the pressing prejudicial noise when having to make judgments about people. Whatever the issue (choosing a supplier, selecting a promotion candidate, making a disciplinary decision) he will always try to give a person a fair hearing. He will always try to collect as much factual evidence as possible and be as objective as possible in analyzing his findings and making a judgment as to what is best for the company and its people. He will try to eliminate subjective influences (Jennie Lester went to the same school as me), and he will never breach his own very strict moral and ethical code.

The Superboss prides himself on his fair and objective judgment, and his people respect him for it.

ACTION TODAY

Re-examine the last important people-decision you made (whether a promotion, a selection, or a disciplinary action). Check through all your thought processes. Note the key factors that influenced your decision, any doubts you had, for example resulting from insufficient information, or whether or not you believed a statement. Now put your hand on your heart and say to yourself, "That was the very best decision I could have made, my judgment was fair and wholly objective, and I did not allow any prejudice to sway me."

Say that every time you make a judgment about anyone (boss, subordinate, supplier, or colleague).

REMEMBER

The judgment of a SUPERBOSS will never be clouded by a flow of alcohol and excellent food. Nor by a smiling face with inviting eyes.

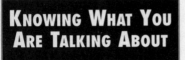

KNOWING WHAT YOU ARE TALKING ABOUT

WHAT A PERSON SAYS IS NOT NECESSARILY A REFLECTION OF WHAT HE OR SHE KNOWS.

Everybody is an expert on employee relations. Or so it seems when they're telling you how to sort out the unions. Not that they've ever carried any responsibility for dealing with unions, nor had to take the lead at negotiations, nor had to make a decision whether to acquiesce to union demands or take the consequences.

I call them the five-second experts. They form strongly held opinions after five seconds' consideration of issues that fall into other people's areas of expertise. You'll hear them holding forth about the company's atrocious advertising, about the poor attitudes of the employees, about why the company should do this or that.

The Superboss listens quietly to the real experts and doesn't pretend he's one. He might ask a question or two of clarification, but he believes it a mark of disrespect to imply to the Advertising Manager that he knows better how to produce advertisements.

When the Superboss makes a statement or expresses an opinion, he knows what he's talking about. He will have gathered the facts previously. He will have taken immense care in analyzing the data and drawing conclusions. If he forms an opinion, it will be as a result of that careful study. You will never hear the Superboss rushing around telling his colleagues, "David Grinstead was a fool to cut expenditure back on that Saudi project. Now look what's happened."

Only the five-second expert would dare apply hindsight on what David Grinstead should have done three months ago. The Superboss wasn't in his shoes, nor anywhere near them, so he'll refuse to give an opinion because he would not know what he's talking about.

ACTION TODAY

Discipline yourself to hold back on the opinions you express, the statements you make. Always ask yourself, "Do I really know what I'm talking about?" If not, keep quiet. Let the experts do the talking.

REMEMBER

You can't be a SUPERBOSS if you don't know what you're talking about.

KNOWING YOUR PEOPLE

IF YOU DON'T KNOW YOUR PEOPLE, YOU KNOW NOTHING.

There are many managers who don't know their people. It's unforgivable. They think they know. Nobody will ever own up to not knowing his or her people, mainly because they don't know they don't know.

What they do know is the surface behavior of their people, the external face of each person. They will see the fronts people put up. But they will see no more. They won't know what lies under that cosmetic smile. They won't know what those polite words hide. They will not know their people.

The Superboss does know. He gets under the surface. He breaks the ice gently by thawing out the start of any conversation, talking about minor unimportant things to begin with. He relaxes the person, is friendly, smiles a lot. He tries hard to put a person at his ease, to unfreeze the initial tension. Then, because he's interested, he gets to know the person by asking unbiased questions about what's going on, how he or she feels about this or that, what his or her concerns are. The Superboss doesn't frown if the person gives a stupid answer, or stutters, or is lost for words. He encourages the person to talk on. The Superboss doesn't interrupt with opinions, doesn't automatically disagree. He waits until the other person finishes because he respects that that person has something important to say, whatever it is.

In that way the Superboss gets to know his people. They will feel he understands, because he's given them time and he's been interested in them. They will feel confident that when a problem arises they can take it to him, because he cares and he knows. And that's enough for them.

ACTION TODAY

Be honest with yourself. Do you really know your people? How often do you call up an individual for a free-ranging informal chat? Ask your secretary to arrange for you to spend an hour individually with a cross-section of your people over the next four weeks (whether or not they report to you). Explain that it is for an informal chat, just to see how things are going.

Once in a while a person will look blank and tell you little, but nine times out of ten they'll tell you ten times as much. You'll get to know them much better.

REMEMBER

Everyone knows who the SUPERBOSS is.

LEADERSHIP WHAT IS THE DIFFERENCE BETWEEN A MANAGER AND A LEADER?

If you don't know the answer to the above question, you're not a leader.

The saddest thing that has happened over recent decades is that many managers have lost their leadership skills. (Of course, many never had any in the first place.)

The ever increasing complexities of the modern business environment with its burgeoning corporate bureaucracies and militant unions, together with a lack of attention to leadership training, has resulted in relatively few leaders in management ranks. All too many managers see their task as one of administration, of pushing paper around, or of progress chasing this and that. Leadership gets lost as the Employee Relations and Head Office "experts" take over.

The Superboss is a leader. He takes command. He knows what he has to achieve and he's out there in front with his team achieving it. Leadership means obtaining the co-operation, consent, and commitment of your team to go to the ends of the earth to achieve your objective. It means getting people to accept your authority to make critical decisions. The Superboss does it by inspiration, by example, by sound judgment. He does it by using all the practices mentioned in this book.

The Superboss is also brave enough to lead the way in making painful decisions. He never shies away from a difficult issue or task. He never shies away from his people if an unpopular decision has to be made. He consults them as he goes. He explains the reasons for his decisions and leads them from there.

The Superboss believes in his people, has conviction, has control. And he has command. He knows where he's going and he leads his people there, because they share that self-same conviction, that self-same belief and they accept his authority, his command, his leadership.

ACTION TODAY

Unless you've been on one in the last year, put yourself on a leadership training course. Call the Training Manager and do it today! If you're Chief Executive, do the same. (You can go out of town so that no one will notice.)

Every manager needs leadership training at least once a year.

REMEMBER

The SUPERBOSS takes command and takes the lead.

| **LEARNING** | # ONCE YOU STOP LEARNING YOU'RE DEAD, OR AT LEAST YOU APPEAR THAT WAY TO YOUR SUBORDINATES. |

One of the worst managers I ever met thought he knew everything. He was very convincing. In fact he almost convinced me he was the world's leading expert on everything.

He thought he knew why his staff were unhappy. (He didn't ask them because he thought he knew better.) He addressed the wrong problem. He paid them more because one or two had moaned about money and that was easy to understand. And when they came out on strike he still didn't learn. So he was removed from his job and he still has to learn why.

All they wanted was a manager who was prepared to learn about what they thought; learn about their suggestions for making improvements in supply, in operational procedures, in administration. Improvements to help them maintain their professional pride in doing an excellent job. He didn't see it that way. Their job was to do their job, not make improvements. That was his job. He knew best, he was the boss, he had nothing to learn from them. In fact they should be learning from him (after all he was always giving them lectures).

The Superboss learns a little every day from the people who know best, the people on the job. He learns from them how to put things right, how to make improvements. He learns about their problems and how he can help. He learns from his own mistakes and those of his team. He respects the knowledge, the experience, the skills, the wisdom of the people around him and draws from it in helping the team perform outstandingly.

The Superboss learns from everyone — his people, his boss, his colleagues, Personnel, and other specialists. He learns from employee representatives, unions, and anyone who is prepared to give genuine honest advice.

The Superboss never stops learning, never stops wanting to learn.

ACTION TODAY

What have you learned today? Write it down. If you can't, you've learned nothing and you're no better a person than you were yesterday, or probably the day before, or last year.

Having written it down, annotate each item of learning with the name of the "teacher," whether that person be a subordinate, colleague, employee representative, or your boss. Then go and see the "teacher" and say how much you appreciated his or her advice; say you found it helpful and learned a lot as a result.

QUESTION

How can you learn to be a SUPERBOSS?

LISTENING — HAVING LEARNED TO TALK, WHO LEARNS TO LISTEN?

People who don't listen are a constant source of irritation. Having listened to them drone on for ten minutes you try to say something and before you complete your sentence they're off again, regardless of what you've tried to say. At meetings they rustle through papers, yawn, pick their noses, and chat idly to the person next to them when someone else is talking. If the subject does interest them they still don't listen, but sit on the edge of their seats eager to interrupt and interject, irrespective of what the last person said.

The Superboss is a keen listener. He is humble enough to know that he has much to learn from what others say. In fact he knows that just by listening when someone comes to him with a problem, perhaps by asking the occasional question, the person will often come up with the solution to his or her problem. The Superboss listens attentively to his team, and goes out of his way to do so, creating frequent opportunities to hear what they have to say, to take into account their views, understand their problems. He lets them have their say first, not commenting until he's clear about their position.

The Superboss, although a superb listener, knows how to handle "wafflers," discreetly drawing their disconnected and extended monologues to a close with a degree of diplomacy the speaker is probably oblivious to.

The Superboss knows that listening is a skill requiring great powers of stamina, self-control, concentration, and understanding. But he knows that on the majority of occasions listening is more productive than talking.

ACTION TODAY

Walk round your department today and ask, "How are things going?" and listen. And if you get a hesitant, non-committal, distant reply probe a little deeper. For example, "How do you find this new computerized supply system?" And listen. You'll learn a lot.

If someone walks in and says: "Boss, I've got a problem with the new set-up in Zone G," just listen. Within five minutes he or she will be telling you the solution, and it'll probably be a better one than you would have suggested had you not listened.

REMEMBER
The SUPERBOSS listens more than he talks.

MAINTAINING FACE

THE PRESENTATION OF FACE IS THE HIGHEST PRIORITY IN MAINTAINING AN EFFECTIVE RELATIONSHIP.

We can all lose face. Perhaps it's when someone scowls at us, swears at us, makes us feel silly, or makes a fool of us.

Losing face often comes from unintentional behavior by the other person. It could be an abrupt end to a telephone call, or a bored look, or not looking you in the eyes. (It's very important to look someone in the eyes.)

No one wants to feel small. Everyone has an inner dignity which he or she wishes to preserve, a dignity based on pride and the awareness that if I am employed by this organization I must have some value and importance to it.

Everyone has to go home after work and face a wife, husband, partner, children, or a friend. When you get home you want to be proud about your work. The last thing you want is to have your tail between your legs because you've lost face among your colleagues, or because someone has slighted you and made you feel small, unwanted, unimportant.

Certain people can brazen it out, maintain a brave face, but for most there will be a deep-down hurt with a sense of rejection and unimportance.

The Superboss is sensitive to people's inner dignity, to their pride. Maintaining face is of the highest priority in preserving his relationship with every person around him. He takes care not to slight anyone, not to make them feel bad. He does his best to let others know that they are as important to the organization as everyone else.

When difficult situations arise, when the facts of poor behavior or poor performance have to be faced, the Superboss does it with dignity, with the object of maintaining face. "Look Richard, you might not like what I'm going to say, but I want to help you. The problem is, the way you're going at the moment makes it difficult for everyone. You're always late, you have a negative attitude, and to be honest your output is way below standard. Now let's talk on how we can get around this problem. . . ." The Superboss wants to help, help maintain the face.

ACTION TODAY

Every time you meet someone today put yourself in their shoes. Ask yourself how he or she reacts when you speak, when you look at them. How would you feel if someone spoke to you like that, looked at you like that? Discipline yourself always to be conscious and aware of what impact you're having on the other person. He or she is employed by the company, he or she is important. Reflect it in the way you face that person.

REMEMBER

The face of a SUPERBOSS is the face of the company.

MANAGING PEOPLE — THERE IS NO EASY ANSWER TO MANAGING PEOPLE SUCCESSFULLY.

It is blatantly obvious that only trained and qualified pilots will be put in command of an airplane.

Human beings display a different order of complexity from an airplane. But they are complex all the same.

Time after time organizations appoint to management and supervisory positions people without experience, skills, training, or potential for the complex task of commanding people.

Would you put an untrained, unqualified person in command of an aircraft? Then why put one in command of people?

The Superboss is a trained and qualified expert in managing people successfully. He will have attended management training courses and benefited greatly from them. If he hasn't had the chance he will have trained himself, seizing any opportunity to learn more about management, to improve his skills in this vital task. The Superboss will be both a management expert and a management enthusiast. Every scrap of experience he will question and learn from. Even as a junior he'll have learned from the way his various bosses managed him, and whether or not that affected his motivation and performance.

The Superboss will always debate managerial excellence with other management enthusiasts, even staying up to midnight to discuss the complexities of managing a dynamic group of people.

What's more the Superboss wouldn't dream of appointing anyone to a management position without having first given that person some relevant training and development, and then carefully monitoring progress and helping the new manager with feedback and counsel.

The Superboss, from all his experience, will evolve his own philosophy of management, his own set of beliefs of what constitutes managerial excellence. He'll develop his own style of management.

The Superboss knows that the process of managing others successfully is difficult and requires an immense amount of time and a high degree of devotion. It requires a great investment, both personally and by the company in management training and development.

ACTION TODAY

Devote some time this evening to writing a short paper (no more than three sides) on what you believe is involved in managing people successfully. Tomorrow circulate the paper to one or two of your colleagues (assuming they're managers), convene a lunchtime session, and debate managerial excellence with them. You'll be surprised at the ideas that come up and what you'll learn.

REMEMBER

The biggest challenge the SUPERBOSS has is to manage his people successfully.

MANAGING TIME

TIME IS A VALUABLE RESOURCE, AND SUCCESS ONLY COMES FROM CAREFULLY PLANNING IT.

Managers are paid for the efficient use of their time. Their contribution is a direct result of how they use it, how they prioritize it.

The Superboss doesn't let the constant stream of extraneous events, demands, telephone calls, and mail dictate the use of his time. He takes control of his time and plans it carefully.

The Superboss doesn't overload his appointment book with too many meetings, or too many trips. The Superboss doesn't allow others to manipulate his appointment book, nor overrule what he has scheduled for it. The last thing the Superboss will do is allow his time to be at the beck and call of his boss.

Managers who are kept running at the behest of their bosses are the worst type. Sometimes even bosses have to wait; normally they understand. The Superboss, for example, would not delay or cancel an interview just because his boss called an urgent meeting.

However, the Superboss plans for a fair amount of "slack" in his appointment book so that he can deal with contingencies. He gets to know how often his boss is likely to place an urgent demand on him, and plans his time accordingly. His people will get to know that the Superboss allocates an hour of free time in his appointment book at 9:00 a.m. and 2:00 p.m. each day, and that's the best time to phone him or see him for five minutes.

The Superboss also plans far in advance, slotting into his appointment book up to a year ahead appraisal dates, formal briefing sessions, progress reviews as well, of course, as vacations. The last thing he'll do is allow his secretary to fill his appointment book and then find that not only does he have to cancel meetings when urgent problems arise, but also that he has allocated no time for appraisals, briefing sessions, and progress reviews.

ACTION TODAY

Prepare an appointment book checklist.

1. Do you have at least 40 percent blank time to deal with matters arising?
2. Do you have the performance appraisals of your team planned twelve months ahead?
3. Have you set aside time for walking the around the department?
4. Are your regular briefing sessions and progress reviews firmly slotted into your appointment book?
5. Have you set aside dates for your vacation?
6. Have you diplomatically explained to your boss and your people your approach to planning and managing your time?

If the answer to any of these questions is "no," plan accordingly and make the necessary changes.

REMEMBER

The SUPERBOSS plans his own time, rather than letting other people plan it for him.

....

MEMOS   MEMOS ARE NO SUBSTITUTE FOR MANAGEMENT.

Memos are a dumb way of communicating. They tend to fall on deaf ears and are symptomatic of the lazy, inept, unthinking, can't-be-bothered manager.

I remember the memo from one of my colleagues which read: "When you have five minutes could we discuss my previous memo on employee relations?" His office was ten yards along the corridor from mine and I saw him at least twice a day. He was always sending me memos like that. I never replied. I always popped along to see him.

Many incompetent paranoid managers write memos for insurance reasons, keeping vast files of "I told you so" documents. But people rarely check back. How could you, with all those reams of paper? Throw them away!

The Superboss only writes memos as a last resort when he knows that face-to-face communication or a quick telephone call will not serve the purpose.

He'll never write memos to express opinions, to issue group reprimands, or to issue minor instructions.

Furthermore the Superboss knows the difference between a memo, a letter, a formal request, a contract, a report, a discussion paper, and a department notice.

The Superboss will react sharply to memo writers who try to earn glory points by copying everyone else in "Haven't I done a good job" memos. He'll take that person aside and explain that there's no glory in writing memos.

The Superboss knows that memos lead to documentary dermatitis and coronaries of the communications system. They lead to psycho-organization disorders such as interdepartmental misunderstandings and de-motivational malpractice. In short, inefficiency.

The Superboss prefers face-to-face, or ear-to-mouth communications, suffering "white-outs" when confronted with too much paper.

ACTION TODAY

Ask your secretary to destroy all memos written or received by you during the last five years.

ACTION TOMORROW

Don't write any memos, nor any replies. Every time you're tempted to write a memo eat an apple and see if you can identify a better way of carrying out that communication — wait for your next team meeting, pick up a telephone, or go and see the person.

REMEMBER

Nobody becomes a SUPERBOSS because of his or her memos.

MISTAKES THE MORE MISTAKES A MANAGER ADMITS THE MORE LIKELY HE OR SHE IS TO BE SUCCESSFUL.

Weak managers see admitting mistakes as a sign of weakness, an admission of failure, an exposure of their own inadequacies. Admitting mistakes makes them feel vulnerable. They worry about loss of credibility in the eyes of their subordinates, their colleagues and, what is worse, their bosses. They fear they will be passed over for promotion, will receive no merit increase. They fear that others will exploit their mistakes, point fingers at them, show them up.

So weak managers cover up their mistakes. They hide them and hope no one will notice. If someone accuses them of making a mistake they become defensive, difficult to pin down. They avoid the subject.

In covering up mistakes the weak managers delude themselves and pass over genuine opportunities for improvement.

Some managers have nothing else to do but wait for other people to make mistakes. Then they're in their element. They point out the mistakes, demand blood, and hover like vultures waiting for the next one to be made.

The Superboss gains strength from admitting mistakes. For a start he knows he can learn from his mistakes and learn from other people in discussing them. Furthermore, in admitting mistakes, he knows that there's little further action people can take. No boss can issue a written warning every time a mistake is made. The cry for blood normally disappears as soon as someone is brave enough and big enough to admit the mistake.

The Superboss also knows how to manage other people's mistakes. The last thing he'll do is kick them for their mistakes; he doesn't manage that way. The first thing he'll do is help the person learn from the mistake. That's mistake management.

In admitting and managing mistakes the Superboss facilitates remedial action and thus creates opportunities for improvement.

ACTION TODAY

This will be an acid test to see if you're a Superboss. Write down five mistakes you've made in the last twelve months. (If you haven't made any you should be Chief Executive by now and running the most profitable operation in the country.)

Prioritize the mistakes and then write down the remedial action you took and what you learned.

If you're brave enough (and this is not compulsory) ask your boss to help you by indicating some of the mistakes you've made this last year. See how your boss's list compares with your own. You might be surprised and learn from it!

REMEMBER

The SUPERBOSS has probably made many more mistakes than you. That's why he's a SUPERBOSS.

MOTIVATION | MONEY, WHIPS, AND MAGIC WANDS ARE USELESS AS MOTIVATIONAL AIDS IN MANAGEMENT.

We all know that the carrot and stick went out of fashion a long time ago. Some people still struggle with money (thinking they can pay people to work harder). Others read about X,Y, Z theories, hierarchy of needs, 3-D, hygiene and grid systems.

The Superboss starts with himself. He knows that if he is not motivated himself, there's no likelihood of his people being motivated. With no boss at his back the Superboss will work hard at weekends to grow beautiful roses. That's self-motivation.

The Superboss will be self-motivated to achieve results that are critical for the company. The actual process of achieving something has an intrinsic satisfaction for him. Pay will not motivate him, although he'll see it as a useful barometer of success. The Superboss will be turned neither on nor off by threats, exhortation, or cajolery. He'll keep his eye on the target and that will be the source of his motivation.

Encouragement and support from his boss will help him along and make him feel good at times. It will keep him going when he feels like giving up. But primarily the Superboss is self-motivated and will only become less motivated if he's constantly held back or unfairly treated.

The Superboss is no different from his people, and he knows it. Their motivation derives from his. His motivation shows through in his enthusiasm for the task at hand, his support for his people, and his excitement about the progress they are making. The Superboss will try very hard to eliminate de-motivators such as poor pay, cramped working environment, inadequate tools, company politics, unsympathetic supervision, and unfair practices. But in the end he knows that motivation is a positive attitude of mind which cannot be manipulated with money.

ACTION TODAY

To be anything like a Superboss you must have your own theory of motivation and, what's more, you must be able to put it into practice. Think about that theory today, check your practices. Ask yourself what motivates you and then ask yourself why it should be any different for your people.

REMEMBER

Self-motivation is the key for the SUPERBOSS.

NEEDS · NO TWO PEOPLE HAVE THE SAME NEEDS. YET MANY MANGERS ASSUME THEY DO.

Needs. We all have them, especially at work. Besides equipment needs (tools, etc.), we have environmental needs (toilets, etc.) and social needs (someone to listen to our moans) as well as personal needs of all types. The need for more money, the need to be praised, the need to be recognized, the need to be consulted, the need to be challenged. The need to get away from it all and do something different.

Needs. We all have them, but they are all different. You cannot sit in your "ivory tower" and blindly assume that the thousand people in the organization have the same needs.

The Superboss gets to know the individual needs of his people — those who need to progress and get promoted; those who need a transfer because they need a change of scenery; those who need a new typewriter; those who need talking to. He discovers their even more complex motivational needs — for frequent praise or encouragement, for the occasional ticking-off, or to be left alone to get on with the job.

The Superboss also makes sure the team knows his needs, for performance, for high standards, for close consultation and communication, for honesty, for openness and straight talking, for people to admit their mistakes before he finds out. The Superboss needs all that and much more. He makes it clear he needs complete commitment and dedication to the task. He needs loyalty to the team and to the company. And to him.

ACTION TODAY

Phone the Personnel Manager and ask him or her to sit down with you and complete a needs analysis for every member of your immediate team. Look at training needs, development needs, motivational needs, environmental needs, physical needs, personal needs, and any other needs you can think of.

Having identified all these, categorize them into those needs which have the most immediate impact on profit and on the person.

Then do something about these priority needs. Take action. Telephone the person and discuss the observed needs with him or her. Once agreed take action to meet the need. Book the training course, buy the new desk, give more praise. The business needs it, he or she needs it, and you need to do it.

REMEMBER

People need a SUPERBOSS to really understand their needs.

MANAGEMENT BY OBJECTIVES (MBO) WAS INVENTED IN THE 1950S. RIGHT OR WRONG?

Wrong!

Management by objectives was invented by Alexander the Great in 340 B.C. at the tender age of 15. He managed to take an expedition to the North of Greece, conquer the rebels, and rename their city Alexandropolis. That was his first objective. Then came Asia Minor.

Management terminology becomes a little confused when it tries to differentiate between objectives, goals, purpose, aims, targets, missions, strategies, and plans of action.

I'll stick with objectives here and define them as the contribution required of a manager. In other words, the key results to be achieved by that person. For a Chief Executive the key results will probably be profit, growth, and, among others, effective employee relations. Each objective, each key result will need to have a specific measure of achievement, quantitative or qualitative.

Beneath the Chief Executive there will be a hierarchy of contributory objectives.

The Superboss will know exactly what his subset of contributory objectives are. They won't be a long list of thirty, but probably between three and eight. He'll constantly have them in mind when leading his team.

They don't necessarily need to be written down, although it sometimes helps. The Superboss and his team will be 100 percent clear about these objectives and especially about their measures of achievement. They will be his objectives and nobody else's. He'll have sole accountability for achieving them. Furthermore he'll know that the company's future success is critically dependent on their achievement.

For the Superboss clear objectives are absolutely essential; he couldn't manage without them.

ACTION TODAY

Examine your objectives and make sure you are 100 percent clear about them. Check with your team. If you don't have any objectives, produce some immediately. Write down what you think they are and show your boss. Get him or her to agree, or modify them as a result of the discussion.

You must have objectives; it's what the company requires of you. You must be clear about them. So must your team. Check today.

ACTION THIS WEEKEND

Dust off your copies of John Humble and Peter Drucker, and scan through these classic books once again. They're essential reading and relate to principles of management that are just as important today as when they were written.

ACTION NEXT WEEK

Review your objectives at your next team meeting.

REMEMBER

No SUPERBOSS can manage without clear-cut objectives.

THERE'S ONLY ONE INTERPRETATION OF AN OPEN-DOOR POLICY: ANY EMPLOYEE CAN WALK THROUGH THAT DOOR WHEN IT'S OPEN.

An open-door policy doesn't mean having your door open all the time. It doesn't mean that only your immediate subordinates can call in when it's open.

It means that anyone in your division, department, or section can come and see you when that door's open. There will be no secretary barring entry, creating obstacles if a junior tries to see you for five minutes.

When his door is literally open the Superboss will give a warm welcome to whoever wants to see him, whatever the issue. If the Superboss doesn't want to see anyone, he'll close the door. If the Superboss has a confidential meeting going on, he'll close the door. If he wants to make a few telephone calls or quietly go through some urgent papers, he'll close the door.

The Superboss, however, will try to keep his door open as much as possible. He'll forbid his secretary to "close off" more than 60 percent of his appointment book. He'll keep the 40 percent free for the open door or for walking around the department. When he's sitting at his desk with an open door he'll use the time profitably by going through the mail, catching up with some of the reading, or making one or two brief telephone calls. If Tina Bailey from Accounts pokes her head round the door, he'll welcome her in with a wave of the arm and give her a couple of minutes.

Although the Superboss keeps his door open frequently, he'll do nothing to undermine the authority of his immediate subordinates. There will be no problem because his immediate team encourages their more junior staff to pop up and see the Superboss occasionally to advise him of progress, to discuss issues and problems with him.

In the view of the Superboss and his team, visibility up, down, and across the organization is welcomed and does not interfere with hierarchical accountability.

ACTION TODAY

Open your door today for at least two hours. Instruct your secretary not to object to anyone coming in. If no one comes in, it's because you're not a Superboss and people are not used to it. In which case you'd better start spreading the message that your door's open and you mean it. Call up one or two people (other than your immediate subordinates) for a chat. Let them know and others know that your door's frequently open.

REMEMBER

For a SUPERBOSS an open door is the opposite of a closed mind.

THE MANAGER WHO OPENS UP IS THE MANAGER WHO OPENS THE WAY TO FINDING THE SOLUTION.

The Superboss opens up to his people, to his boss, to his colleagues, to his immediate team.

He knows that the more he "closes up," the less people will trust him. The Superboss likes to open up problems, rather than push them below the surface. Often the problem is no more than a bad feeling he has about something or somebody.

If he feels unhappy about the way Annette Marks has been approaching her work, he'll open up and tell her just that. "I want to be open and honest with you Annette; I feel unhappy about the way things are going at the moment." He'll try to explain why.

If he's disappointed about the lack of progress in installing a new wash unit in Bay 3, he'll open up and tell his team.

The process of opening up to his people reveals the Superboss's emotions. It shows that when it comes to emotion and intellect, he's not all intellect; that when it comes to heart and mind he's not all mind. By revealing his feelings the Superboss opens up his heart, and shows some emotion.

He opens up not to moan, not to undermine his people's confidence in him, not to disillusion them. He opens up because he wants to help his people.

The Superboss also knows that if he opens up to his people, tells them how he feels, it's more likely they will open up to him. By opening up the Superboss accesses problems quickly and resolves them.

ACTION TODAY

Set aside half an hour at coffee time and call in a couple of your team. Open up to them about your concerns, about one or two problems that are bugging you, about how you feel things are progressing. Seek their advice and help.

Encourage them to open up on how they feel about certain things.

Your relationship with them will improve and it's possible you'll open your way to solving that nagging problem.

REMEMBER

Open up to a SUPERBOSS and he'll help you.

 OPPORTUNITIES, OPPORTUNITIES, OPPORTUNITIES! WHY DO SO MANY MANAGERS MISS THEM?

Life is full of opportunities; that's what makes it so exciting. Don't blink now, you might be missing one!

Life at work is full of opportunities, no matter how good, how bad your company. Even in the perfect company dynamic change creates opportunity.

Managers miss opportunities because they're blind, or to be fair they have not trained themselves to look for them. Vertical tracks do not lead to opportunities, and when you've followed them all your career the process of looking laterally for opportunities does not come easily.

The Superboss seizes an opportunity a day — an opportunity to motivate a junior supervisor by asking him or her to represent the company at a conference in Geneva; the opportunity to slash the distribution budget by replanning delivery schedules and reducing transport costs; the opportunity to bring his team together for a game of golf on Friday afternoon; the opportunity to meet Rob Hadon at Redland's and regain their business.

The Superboss knows that the best way to identify and seize opportunities is not to let the "management routines" start managing him. Routines are ruts which lead to predictable results. Routines are the antithesis of entrepreneurial thinking.

Large unwieldy organizations, like dinosaurs, eventually die because they develop rigidly bureaucratic routines and regimes which stifle the entrepreneurial quest for opportunities and initiative, let alone survival.

The Superboss can beat a dinosaur any day in making a profit, in getting his people to seize opportunities, be creative, and make progress.

ACTION TODAY

Look at your appointment book, at your mail, at all those boring things you have planned for today. Look again and immerse yourself, even wallow, in that mire of bureaucracy and imminent committee meetings. Think only of the routines, the ruts and the boring bits. Now think of green fields, flowers, rivers, and distant mountains. The next thought that comes into your head should be an opportunity.

If it isn't, think again. And if that doesn't work, think again (always thinking of the boring bits first, then the green fields, the flowers, the rivers, and the distant mountains).

Eventually you will think of an opportunity to do something special for your company and your team.

REMEMBER

The opportunity for you to become a SUPERBOSS exists right now. (Yes! This very minute.)

OVERVIEW — WITHOUT THE OCCASIONAL OVERVIEW YOU CAN HAVE NO PROPER VIEW.

When the rush is on, when the pressure mounts, it's not easy to step back and take an overview. But it is vital.

The manager under pressure will only have a limited view. He'll see the surface problems and arrive at surface solutions. If the engineers have stopped work, if the production line is at a halt for the third time this week, if there's an irate customer on the line complaining about late delivery, if the Chairman is demanding to see him to explain what's going on, and if poor Tenny Kai wants to see him on a personal matter, then the last thing the typical manager might think about is taking an overview. But the Superboss will. He'll step back and try to put the problems into perspective. By doing so he'll take control, rather than let events control him. That way he'll avoid a cosmetic solution. He'll decide to devote more time to getting to the heart of the engineers' problem. He'll decide to see that irate customer over lunch. Furthermore, he'll arrange to have a quiet half hour with the Chairman to chew the cud with him on the problems. And he won't forget poor Tenny Kai. He'll probably decide to see her first.

And at the weekend while playing golf the Superboss will take another overview, looking back at the events of the past week. Once a month he'll sit down for some deep thinking. By taking frequent overviews the Superboss maintains a good perspective of the ever changing scene at his workplace.

PAIN — THERE IS NO PLEASURE IN MANAGEMENT WITHOUT PAIN.

Things don't come easily in management. For every satisfying decision you make, there always seems to be an equally painful one.

In a harsh competitive world you can do your best and still not do well enough, whether as a company, a manager, or a junior employee.

The Superboss takes no delight in making painful decisions, but at least he will make them. Weaker managers will shy away from them.

The Superboss will only have to look at market trends and the downturn in figures to know that economies will be necessary. He will explore every conceivable way to avoid having those economies adversely affecting his people. But in the end he will make the painful decision that jobs must go.

The Superboss will look at the way poor Tom Reuben has just not been able to cope as Quality Control Manager, despite all the help, advice, and encouragement given to him. In the end the Superboss will reluctantly conclude that Tom Reuben will have to be removed from the job.

It pains the Superboss to bring up the subject of poor performance with a loyal member of his team, but he will. It pains the Superboss to reject nine thoroughly good candidates for a key job (when the tenth was only marginally better), but he will. It pains the Superboss to argue with his boss and have to accept a crazy decision, but he will.

In the end the Superboss will always take the pain rather than avoid the problem.

ACTION TODAY

Shut your door. Ask your secretary to leave you alone for half an hour. Make a critical review of all those difficult situations around you. Be honest. Is there one decision you're shying away from? Accept the pain and make the decision.

REMEMBER

The SUPERBOSS will not avoid a painful decision, but in implementing the decision he'll try to avoid the pain.

PARTICIPATION	# PARTICIPATION IS THE KEY TO COMMITMENT.

This is a controversial subject. Workplace democracy. A manager is not a manager unless he or she has sole accountability for making specified decisions.

The process of bringing people together round the table to participate in decision-making can be cumbersome and time consuming. It does secure commitment, however, and is well worthwhile if all participants have the same underlying interest and can contribute some expertise towards making the decision. It will fail if there are conflicting selfish interests and the participants are not expert in the issue under consideration.

The Superboss makes decisions. He'll encourage interested parties to participate in the process, but if it's 51 of one and 49 of the other he'll make a decision and risk upsetting the 51.

But it's rarely like that. Wherever possible the Superboss will try to make his decision in accordance with the consensus view. However, when he has to go against that view he'll explain his reasons why and try to help the participants understand.

To encourage participation on a regular basis the Superboss will share his thoughts with his people, will share his ideas, his enthusiasms, and also his concerns. Equally he will try very hard to share their thoughts, their ideas, enthusiasms, and concerns. Participation and sharing is a two-way process of giving, and giving of yourself. It is a continuing process that the Superboss will undertake informally every day. Participation is the antithesis of taking, of exploiting, of demanding, of imposing.

By participating and contributing to a decision employees are most likely to become committed to that decision.

In the final analysis, however, accountability cannot be shared (otherwise you fire the whole group if things go wrong). No matter how much participation and sharing there is, the decision in the end will be that of the Superboss.

ACTION TODAY

Stroll around your area, share your thoughts with everyone you meet. Share with them your biggest concerns, your ideas about getting some key problems resolved. Invite them to share their ideas with you. Encourage them to participate in the resolution of some of the problems exposed and in some of the decisions that have to be made.

ACTION NEXT WEEK

Gather together for an informal meeting a cross-section of people in your area (representing all sections and levels).

Invite them to participate in a decision-making discussion about improvements at their place of work.

Listen carefully. Share with them your thoughts on the ideas they suggest. Try to obtain some consensus. Then make a decision and follow through.

Don't bypass your direct reports. Invite them to join in too. You might ask an employee relations specialist to chair the meeting.

REMEMBER

The SUPERBOSS encourages his people to participate in making decisions affecting them, because more often than not they know better than he does what decision should be made.

PAY THE LEAST OF A MANAGER'S WORRIES SHOULD BE PAY.

You cannot buy people with money. You cannot buy your way out of people problems.

Many unions have done a great disservice to their members by translating every employee relations problem into a money problem. "We won't handle dirty cargo unless you pay us 'dirty' money." "We won't use this new equipment unless you pay 'new equipment pay.'" The men go on strike, the operation stops, the management backs down and pays "dirty" money or "new equipment pay." In management's view (and the union knows it) it's cheaper to pay an extra week's wages as "dirty" money than lose three months' revenue.

The jungle grows through bad management and mercenary unions.

The Superboss takes a straight forward view of pay. "Pay as well as you can, within reason, and then get on with the job." The Superboss insists on a fair and equitable level of compensation for his people. If the company can afford it, he'll fight for his people to be paid well. If the company can't afford it, he'll convince his people why.

The Superboss suffers no nonsense with back-door payments, such as unnecessary overtime, pseudo-allowances, or special one-time bonuses. He believes in paying the best rate possible for the job. He believes in high pay because that's the best way to get high performance. With average pay you tend to get average performance.

The Superboss doesn't leave it to the Personnel Department to make pay decisions. He'll fight his case with Personnel, and with the Chief Executive if necessary. He wants to get the pay issue out of people's mind. He wants them to forget it and get on with the job.

The one thing he won't forget to do, however, is personally hand the pay slip or pay packet to each member of his team. It's an opportunity for personal contact and to strengthen the bond.

Personal handing over of pay slips is something the Superboss encourages throughout his area.

ACTION TODAY

Form an opinion. Does the company pay your people (10, 100, or 1,000) well? Take into account the marketplace, company performance, cost of living trends, internal relativities, and so on. If the answer is "yes," forget about pay and get on with the job, perhaps going to see Personnel for an informal chat next time the pay round approaches.

If the answer is "no," collect the hard facts, prepare your case carefully, and as a Superboss go and fight the battle.

ACTION FOR PAY DAY

Arrange with the payroll department that all your team's pay slips or packets are sent to you and that you will personally deliver each one, taking the opportunity for a brief chat at the same time.

REMEMBER

If the SUPERBOSS doesn't fight the pay battle for his people, the union will.

PEOPLE COME FIRST

WHERE WOULD WE BE WITHOUT PEOPLE? THEY MUST COME FIRST. THEY SHOULD BE AN ORGANIZATION'S MOST PRIZED ASSET.

Profit through people, not at the expense of them. Consider people as a prized asset, not as a variable cost.

This is a theme that runs consistently through this book. It is a key theme for the Superboss. People must come first, every time.

People come first in the allocation of the Superboss's time, first on his priority list.

That fact is so obvious that it's amazing that so many managers put other things first; they neglect to spend time with their people; neglect to take an interest in them; neglect to give attention to selecting them, to training them, to encouraging and supporting them, to helping them, and to consulting them. They are managers who have more important things to do than fight battles on behalf of their people. You'll probably see these managers spending hours pouring over new product designs, financial analyses, detailed project reports, and other things.

The Superboss knows that if he doesn't put his people first, they won't put him and the company first. Putting them first doesn't mean mouthing fine words like "We are a people-caring company" or "We have a listening management." It means fine action. The Superboss puts his people first by fixing their parking problems, by sorting out the heating in the office, by giving priority to resolving a pay parity problem, by listening to their troubles and helping resolve them.

ACTION TODAY

Examine how you allocate your time. Do you have a tendency to say to yourself, "I haven't time to take a stroll around the department today; I must get through this back-log of mail"? Do you prefer to get sucked into meetings with your boss rather than see

Debbie Nash when she's got a prickly problem? How often do you initiate informal chats with people throughout your department? Would you prefer that some of those intractable people problems go away so that you could concentrate on completing that study on product reliability your boss called for?

Starting today, give high priority to the people issues. Take a stroll around your department, initiate a series of informal chats with some junior staff. Try to crack some of those intractable people problems:"Yes, I must confront John Peters rather than let him go on stirring up trouble."

REMEMBER

The SUPERBOSS never lets his people down, because he always puts them first.

PERCEPTION	## PERCEPTIONS HAVE A FAR GREATER INFLUENCE ON PEOPLE'S ATTITUDES AND BEHAVIOR THAN THE ACTUAL FACTS.

I remember seeing a politician recently on television. There had been some debacle in which the government had been accused of not listening to its own members. The politician kept on saying, "But we are a listening government." The perception of the audience and the questioners was different. Every time he repeated the statement there was derisory laughter.

The company might say, "We can't afford a pay increase," and present financial figures to demonstrate this. The perception might be otherwise. It might be that if the company can afford to move to a new office block, if it can afford an expensive new advertising campaign, if it can afford lavish entertainment for visiting dignitaries, then it can afford a pay increase.

A company might say, "We are a people-caring company" and then assign the lowest budgetary priority to resolving a parking problem that has been bugging the staff for years.

Fine words cannot influence perception, only fine action.

The Superboss is very much concerned with the perceptions of his people. He's concerned that if the company exhorts people to improve efficiency, that they perceive it as being not only necessary but feasible.

Perceptions derive not from facts or words, but from what people actually do. The Superboss knows that for perceptions to be favorable a manager must demonstrate total consistency between the words he utters and the decisions and actions he takes.

ACTION TODAY

List the three most important things you have tried to convey to your people over the last four weeks.

Call your Employee Relations Manager and ask him or her to get around and talk to your people. Ask him or her to check their perceptions of what they see as important.

Then compare notes. You might be surprised.

REMEMBER

When the SUPERBOSS cries "wolf," there really is a wolf.

POLITICS — THERE'S NO PROFIT IN MANAGEMENT POLITICS.

Politics has a bad name and rightly so. When you're out to catch votes you'll say and do anything to be popular, and suppress and hide anything which may have the reverse effect. But people aren't that stupid, and tough painful action and blunt words can often win votes. People see through syrupy smiles and become suspicious of those who don't tell them the "bottom line."

The Superboss plays no political games, is not out to win the popularity stakes. The Superboss doesn't try to outshine and show up his colleagues, nor drop them in the mire. Nor does he paint things black and then suddenly turn them white when he becomes responsible.

The Superboss doesn't try to score points, nor impress the Chairman with his superlative verbal skills. The Superboss doesn't sacrifice other people to cover his own inadequacies, nor does he look for scapegoats when things go wrong.

The Superboss doesn't act behind his boss's back, nor those of his people. The Superboss is not a student of Machiavelli nor does he wish to emulate him.

The Superboss keeps his leadership style honest and straight, speaking his mind in a considered and responsible way. He fights for his company and for his people and is prepared to risk sticking his neck out to do so. His preoccupation is with getting good results rather than scoring political points.

ACTION TODAY

Make a New Year's resolution (even if it's June 23) that you will cease to have anything to do with internal politics within the company. You might react in horror, believing that unless you play company politics your survival (let alone promotion) prospects will be greatly reduced. Well, if you're anything like a Superboss, your conscience will be more important than your career. Do you really want to work for a company that is going to sacrifice you unless you play its political games?

Concentrate on the task at hand, forget about politics, and think about achieving some excellent results.

REMEMBER

For the SUPERBOSS there's no greater waste of time than internal politics.

POSITIVENESS — YOU HAVE TO BE POSITIVE TO MANAGE PEOPLE SUCCESSFULLY.

Never say no! Saying no is the most negative thing a manager can do, and I'm afraid many of them do it frequently. You might think the corollary is to say yes all the time. Far from it.

In making decisions the Superboss exercises reason and tries to persuade people with it, or conversely they persuade him.

The Superboss is reluctant to reject anything, whether it be an idea, a proposal, a recommendation, a suggestion, or a request for five minutes of his time.

The Superboss will always try to give a positive response, will always try to accept someone's recommendation, will always try to help. He'll disagree with a person from time to time, but the process of disagreement will not be a negative act but a process of constructive criticism and help.

When you have a team working smoothly and cohesively together, all pointing in the same direction and working hard to achieve a desired goal, any negative decision, statement, or act will in effect retard progress by channeling some of the team's energy away from the goal.

In being positive the Superboss will keep that energy harnessed in one direction only. While he might not agree with a request for an additional clerk in Geraldine Shear's section, he'll present to her the options in having to make the decision: "What would you do Geraldine, if you were in my shoes? Go over budget with an additional clerk, or perhaps see if there's another way of getting the additional work done?" The resulting decision will be the most positive for the company and its people.

ACTION TODAY

Take a large box. Stick a label on it and mark it with large letters: "Negativity Box."

Every time you are tempted to make a negative decision look at the box. If you do succumb, make a written note of that negative decision, no matter how trivial, and put it in the box. At your next team meeting ask your people to estimate how many slips of paper are inside that box. If you are a SUPERBOSS, every team member will get the right answer every time.

That's being positive! Every one a winner!

QUESTION
Is your SUPERBOSS positively the best?

PRAISE — PRAISE THE MANAGER WHO PRAISES HIS STAFF.

Managers often blame their staff for what is going wrong in their division. In my humble opinion it is an unforgivable sin, yet I've come across it frequently. I've heard managers complain about those silly little girls who are not interested one bit in what's going on. Or those villains, the industrial workers, who'll screw the company for everything they can get. Such managers will even complain about individual members of their team.

In the Superboss's view, if he can't praise someone in his team, that person shouldn't be a member of it. If he can't praise the team itself, it's because he's hopeless as a team leader.

The Superboss has faith in his people. He knows they give of their best and he'll make a point of praising them for it.

For the Superboss one of life's great satisfactions is to find something good and give praise. For example, he might phone in from outside one day and get a warm friendly response from the telephone operator who doesn't know it's him.

The next day he'll go and see Bettie Fowler, the switchboard supervisor, and praise her and the team. When he finds that Rikki Powell in purchasing has secured a two percent price reduction from a major supplier, he'll give high priority to praising her for her contribution.

The praise of a Superboss is never uncritical, always genuine. He doesn't give praise for praise's sake, or use it as a superficial motivational cosmetic in order to make a person feel good, irrespective of performance. His praise must be earned, for he'll only praise real contribution.

ACTION TODAY

Ask your secretary to bring in a nice new notebook. Get some art supplies and print on the cover "Praise Book." Take each clean page and write at the top the date for the next 50 consecutive working days (or 100 if the notebook is a fat one).

Your task now is to make an effort each day to praise at least three people, whether it be your immediate reportees or people in their teams. You must make a note of who you praise and why. It can be for minor things (your secretary has cleaned out the top drawer of your desk) or major things (your team exceeded sales quota for the fifth consecutive month). The praise must be genuine and for a real contribution to the company and its people.

REMEMBER

When the SUPERBOSS praises someone, he means it.

PRIDE — HE WHO HAS NO PRIDE SHOULD HAVE NO JOB. TAKE PRIDE IN YOUR PEOPLE; IT IS YOUR JOB.

It is a question of personal honor. There is no honor in not giving of your best at work.

Many people have a thousand reasons for not giving of their best. They feel exploited or underpaid. They feel their working conditions are not good enough, that the company takes them for granted, that they're treated like machines instead of people. They feel that career progression is governed by a political rat race and is unfair. They feel let down by the company, discriminated against. They have no pride in what they're doing. And it follows that the company has no pride in them.

The Superboss is a proud man. He holds his head up high and speaks highly of his people. He tells his family, his neighbors, his friends how great his people are. He is proud of what he has done for them; proud of the way he has improved their working conditions; proud of the way they have all been trained; proud of the way so many of them have been promoted out of his department.

Most of all he is proud of what they have done for him, what they have achieved.

His team is proud too. They are proud to work for a Superboss, proud of his reputation, proud of his leadership. They take pride in all aspects of their work: the quality of the product and the service, the housekeeping, the team spirit. They take pride in achieving excellent results and beating the competition.

The Superboss's pride will be hurt sometimes. It will be hurt when his people tell him that the parking problem he promised to sort out still hasn't been sorted. It will be hurt when he learns his team has slipped three days on a delivery to Blanchard's. It will be hurt when the trusted Jon Andersen is caught thieving. It will be hurt when he forgets to call in and see Ina Ling as promised. But when his pride is hurt he will always take action to redress it.

ACTION TODAY

You must be proud to be a manager. If you're not proud, stay at home and think very deeply about it.

Be positive. What do you really feel proud about at work? What do you really feel proud about as a manager? What pride do you take in your people? Do you show pride in them? How? Do you take pride in your results, their results? If you can answer these questions positively, hold your head up high and go to work.

REMEMBER

You can tell a SUPERBOSS by the pride he takes in his people and their results.

PRINCIPLES EVERY MANAGER MUST HAVE A CLEAR FRAMEWORK OF PRINCIPLES WITHIN WHICH HE MANAGES.

You never know where you stand with a manager who lacks a clearly defined set of management principles. It's not that they are dishonest or devious, it's just that they tend to be arbitrary in their decisions, in the views they formulate. Managers who lack principles tend to change their minds frequently, tend to blow with the wind, tend to be nice to you when they want something and ignore you at other times.

Managers who lack management principles are managers who don't think. They do what they're told. They say the first thing that comes into their head. They push the paper around, take the telephone calls, and are deft at passing on problems to someone else. Such managers are often manipulative, not only manipulating people but manipulating words. They avoid commitment by talking their way out of everything, presenting to the uninitiated a glossy facade of management effectiveness and understanding. For such managers expediency becomes a substitute for principle.

The Superboss is a man of principle. Over the years he has carefully thought through the basic principles of managing people successfully and developed his own personal framework. That framework supports him every minute of his management career. It forms the basis for every decision he makes about people, his behavior towards them, and the initiatives he takes. His principles are those of any superb manager. They are based on openness, honesty, commitment, co-operation, positiveness, support, people-caring, profit-mindedness, and many others. In fact they are the principles which form the basis for this book.

ACTION TODAY

This is an evening job. After dinner (don't drink any wine) diplomatically ask your partner to leave you alone for an hour or two "to do some thinking." Turn down the lights and place on your stereo a Mozart piano concerto (or whatever, your choice). Shut your eyes and search deep into your heart. Look at your management principles. In all conscience are you 100 percent clear about them? Don't be complacent. Don't con yourself with a quick easy answer. (You can jump into bed later; it's probably being kept warm for you.) Ask yourself again: "What are the principles upon which I manage my people on a day-by-day basis?" When you have a genuinely honest answer, ask yourself two difficult questions: "Do I carry the conviction to apply these principles? Do I sometimes allow expediency to displace my principles?" Think carefully, think honestly, think twice. Re-establish and re-apply your principles; it's the most important thing you can do. Then drink a glass of wine with your partner and go to bed.

PRIORITIES

PRIORITIES ALWAYS COME FIRST, SO IF YOU WANT TO COME FIRST, DECIDE ON YOUR PRIORITIES.

Working out your priorities is a continuous process. The Superboss is doing it all the time.

To achieve his profit objectives, to achieve what he wants for his people the Superboss is continually reviewing how to deploy his valuable resources — the time and efforts of his people as well as his own, the money in his budget, the physical equipment at his disposal. The needs of his customers, his company, and his people will change day by day and therefore the Superboss's priorities will need to be reviewed day by day.

He might sit down quietly at eight o'clock each morning, before anyone comes into his office, and review his priorities for the day. He might sit down on the weekend, perhaps for half an hour before lunch, and review his priorities for the coming week or month. He might decide to spend less time on training and more on an urgent quality problem; to deploy more resources to complete that investment study on the two new locations in the Northwest. He will realize that he has neglected poor old Joe Quinn these last few weeks and it has now become a priority to devote some time to him.

The Superboss will be constantly reviewing priorities with his own boss, whether he be the Chief Executive or the Production Manager on line 4. He will also review priorities with his team at his regular meeting with them. In the end decisions on priorities will be his, but he will involve those around him as much as possible.

The Superboss knows that effective prioritizing leads to profits and success for the company and its employees.

ACTION TODAY

List your priorities for (a) today, (b) tomorrow, (c) next week, (d) next month. Try to determine what is most important for the company and your people in the allocation of your time and their time, as well as in the allocation of money.

Having listed your priorities, go and see your boss for an informal chat. Review with him or her (c) and (d) above. Having confirmed these priorities with your boss, discuss them with your team at the next regular meeting.

Don't forget that giving time to your people is a high priority.

REMEMBER

The priority of the SUPERBOSS is people, and consequently performance and profit.

PROBLEM SOLVING

MOST MANAGERS ARE EXPERT AT STATING PROBLEMS, FEW AT SOLVING THEM.

A consultant once advised me: "As soon as you identify a problem you own it." But . . . "I can't motivate my people because the company's pay policy is a real problem;" "The problem is the company doesn't allow us to manage, we don't even have the authority to buy a new computer;" "The problem is Employee Relations, they're so bureaucratic. I get a constant stream of documentation from them. I wish I could get on and do my real job."

There used to be a little plaque you could buy to put on the wall of your office which said, "The bad manager finds 48 reasons why a problem cannot be solved. The good manager finds 48 ways of solving that problem."

If you can't solve a problem, forget it. It's not worth worrying about. If it's going to affect you, worry about it and do something.

The Superboss gets off his behind and gets to the heart of the problem and does his best to solve it. If there really is a problem with company pay policy, he'll make a case to his boss and to Employee Relations. It'll be a persuasive case, well researched, well presented, and aimed at convincing the decision-makers that unless there is a change there will be immense damage to the company. If the problem is supervisory training the Superboss will demonstrate to his boss the effect the lack of training is having (low efficiency, poor safety record, low morale, high employee turnover, too many customer complaints). He'll convince his boss an investment in training is well worthwhile. He'll also persuade him or her to delegate more authority to him to avoid wasting time on computer issues.

If the Superboss sees a problem, he doesn't let it rest. He sets out to solve it, even if it appears that the solution lies in the hands of others. If the problem impacts him, it's his problem. He'll convince the other people.

ACTION TODAY

This is where, once and for all, you stop the moaning and groaning. Purge your mind of all your management problems. Divide them into two lists:

1. Those you can do something about.
2. Those you can do nothing about.

Destroy the second list and never refer to those problems again. Now set about solving the problems in the first list. You'll be amazed at your ability to persuade people. Don't give up; you will need to persist.

REMEMBER

If the SUPERBOSS can't solve a problem the first time, he'll try a second and then a third time. He'll keep on trying, a thousand times if necessary, until he solves it.

PROFIT

LONG-TERM BUSINESS SUCCESS CAN ONLY COME FROM A FAIR BALANCE BETWEEN PEOPLE AND PROFIT. ONE MUST THEREFORE PROFIT THROUGH PEOPLE, NOT AT THEIR EXPENSE.

You cannot separate people from profit, nor profit from people. The worst managers are those who see people as costs. The lower the costs, the higher the profits. The logic being that if you cut down on wages and numbers of people you force up profits.

Fallacy! People should not be numbered in the profit and loss account.

The Superboss sees his people as a key asset in his balance sheet, an asset that generates profit. While never losing sight of profit, he devotes much energy and resource to developing that asset. The Superboss doesn't sell his people short, doesn't run them down to make more profit. The Superboss invests in his people.

But he knows there's little charity in business. The Superboss always has an eye on the "bottom line," never loses sight of it. His quirks, his eccentricities, his occasional indulgences never cloud his view of the profit objective.

The Superboss never scrimps on paper clips, electric light, or travel expenses. Nor does he scrimp on having the best people in his team, for only they can produce maximum revenue and profit.

Although the Superboss will tolerate the occasional indulgence (that's only human), he will not allow profligacy. The Superboss will indulge a trainee sales person who profits from expense allowances when away from base, but will not indulge the senior executive who throws wild parties at the company's expense to entertain the Pavrottis from Palermo. (Who? From where?)

Every decision the Superboss makes is geared to helping the company profit from having the very best people. People and profit are inextricably linked, and he never loses sight of either.

ACTION TODAY

At 5:30 this evening enter in the profit and loss account the pre-cise monetary contribution you made for the company in the last eight hours. If it is a profit figure you are perfectly entitled to come to work again tomorrow morning. (No other answer is acceptable. Excuses are out of the question.)

REMEMBER

The SUPERBOSS never loses sight of profit, nor of his people's contribution to it.

PROMOTION | THE BEST MANAGERS PROMOTE THEIR PEOPLE RATHER THAN THEMSELVES.

For the Superboss his greatest sacrifice is his greatest pleasure — to get the very best member of his team promoted to another part of the company.

You must have heard it in those dull dispirited organizations where nobody ever progresses: "My boss is blocking my promotion," or "My boss thinks I'm indispensable," or "My boss is holding me back." In such companies promotion opportunities are few and far between, and when they do occur the wrong people are perceived to get the job, the right ones are passed over and grieve that they didn't even have a fair chance.

The Superboss will create a dynamic organization in which promotion opportunities occur frequently. He'll search for them. The last thing he'll do is get all his people's jobs upgraded in order to simulate promotion, but he'll do everything possible to create genuine promotion opportunities. He will assign senior people to projects, or other parts of the company so that openings can be created to bring on and promote up-and-coming juniors.

The Superboss will encourage others to compete for promotion. He will encourage them to acquire broad experience, achieve results, develop their skills so that they are in the best position to pursue opportunities. He'll encourage his "indispensable" finance manager to apply for a transfer to another division, knowing that if this takes place at least three promotion opportunities will occur. (When it comes to promotion nobody is "indispensable" to the Superboss.)

The Superboss will ensure that all suitable candidates are given a fair and equal opportunity to obtain a career advance. Promotion decisions will be arrived at in a rigorously objective manner after painstaking consideration of each candidate.

ACTION TODAY

If nobody's been promoted from your area within the last year, you're a failure, and so is the company. Start now and create some genuine promotion opportunities. Recognize that for each person promoted nine others will be disappointed. Even so the prospects will encourage competition and development.

If you can't identify a promotion opportunity for one of your people within the next three months, either resign or ask for a transfer. That will create one.

REMEMBER

For the SUPERBOSS getting his people promoted is the hallmark of success.

PUSH FOR EXCELLENCE

IF A MANAGER DOESN'T PUSH FOR EXCELLENCE, WHAT DOES HE OR SHE PUSH FOR?

Some managers don't push. In fact they allow others to push them around — their bosses, the unions, their colleagues, their people. A manager might even get a reputation as being a "pushover" for giving people whatever they want.

The Superboss doesn't sit back and wait to be pushed. He's out there in front pushing for excellence, for higher standards of performance, for an even bigger contribution by his team to the company's profit.

The Superboss is able to push hard because he's very clear about what he has to achieve and very confident about the capabilities of his people. He'll push them for additional sales revenue, for additional production output, for excellent customer service, for excellent quality, for excellent housekeeping. He'll push them for an excellent safety record and for excellent employee relations, accepting only a positive, cohesive, co-operative style of team work.

The Superboss pushes for excellence, recognizes it and rewards it with praise, giving constructive feedback to those who are not quite there. To achieve excellence the Superboss selects only the very best people and ensures they receive the very best training and development. When his team are around the table he'll make sure they are very clear about the standards of excellence he wants them to achieve.

The Superboss pushes for excellence because he knows that every person in his area wants to be proud of an excellent performance and furthermore wants the support of a Superboss to achieve it.

ACTION TODAY

Complete on one sheet of paper an "Excellence Analysis." Draw two columns. On the left list all the things where your team and your people have demonstrated their excellence. Don't be afraid to put down items of individual excellence.

In the right hand column list "Opportunity Areas" where you feel your team are not quite achieving excellence. (There must be some opportunity; they can't be that excellent!) On this occasion do not list individual opportunity areas (take those up separately). If you have no idea of what constitutes excellence in your area you're already an abysmal failure.

ACTION NEXT WEEK

Convene your team and discuss with them your "Excellence Analysis." Modify it as appropriate. Then go out, you and your team, and really push for excellence.

REMEMBER

The SUPERBOSS doesn't expect perfection, but he does expect excellence.

....

| **QUESTION** | THERE ARE NO EASY ANSWERS IN MANAGEMENT, ONLY DIFFICULT QUESTIONS. |

If you know all the answers you probably haven't asked the right questions. In this competitive world there are no easy answers as to how to make profit, how to achieve really effective employee relations. The scene changes daily; new factors arise, organizations change, people move on, sales drop, unexpected orders come in, new competition appears and so on. Even on the shopfloor, where a routine production operation exists, things are changing all the time; absenteeism goes up, the standard of house-keeping goes down, suddenly a fault will occur on a packing machine you haven't had a problem with for five years.

The Superboss is alert to all these events, has an inquisitive mind, is always asking questions: "Why this? Why that?" Not that he doesn't trust his people, not that he wants to interfere. He just wants to know what's going on. By asking the right question at the right time he might come up with the answer that has eluded everyone else, might just find a way through when nobody else could.

In fact the Superboss has a talent, some would say instinct, for getting to the root of the problem in almost no time. The Superboss has that canny ability to listen carefully when a serious problem arises, ask one or two apparently innocuous questions and then intuitively point towards the solution.

The Superboss spends much of his time diplomatically questioning people: "Why didn't we use the ten-ton truck for that trip? Why didn't Tubby Wagg show up for work yesterday? Why have we shut down that cooling chamber three times in the last week? Why aren't you smiling today, Sandra?"

The Superboss is always questioning his team, challenging them, keeping them on their mettle. Not because he doesn't trust them, but because he knows that without questioning people tend to become slovenly in their judgments, narrow in their outlook.

No one person can see everything. The Superboss, with his well directed questions, helps his people and himself to see more.

ACTION TODAY

Take your normal walk around and discipline yourself to question any single thing you do not understand: "Why is that container lying unused in the corner? Why are those men sitting talking nervously in the canteen? Why haven't we had a reply from Roseland's?"

You will expect the people responsible to know the answers. If they don't, then perhaps you can help them. If you really know the answers, don't ask the questions.

REMEMBER

The SUPERBOSS knows that to answer to his own boss he first has to ask the right questions.

RECOGNITION — TO RECOGNIZE MANAGERIAL EXCELLENCE IS TO RECOGNIZE POTENTIAL PROFIT.

In a company I once knew there was a huge management problem. At one stage the managers nearly rebelled because they felt the directors were not consulting them on key issues, for example their own pay. "You spend hours with the unions negotiating pay, but you never even bother to talk to us managers about our own pay."

A consultant was commissioned to undertake a survey of how the managers perceived the company and its directors. The results were alarming. Seventy percent of the managers were not clear about their jobs and objectives but, what was worse, 80 percent felt the contribution they made was not recognized by the board. It was not only recognition through pay and promotion, although that was important. It was actual recognition by saying "thank you" when a manager had pulled out all the stops on an urgent job.

Unfortunately it was a company that recognized fine words, but failed to recognize the real contribution made by each manager towards results.

The Superboss has an eye for excellence, for good performance, for the exact contribution each of his subordinates makes. He ensures that that contribution is recognized by the company. It helps, of course, to have clear objectives and that was part of the problem I referred to. Because there were no clear objectives for any one manager it was difficult, if not impossible, to recognize achievement.

The Superboss knows that his people want to be recognized for what they're worth. After all, if the company values them by paying a good salary, why shouldn't it recognize them by valuing the contribution they make? People need to know they earn their salary.

Recognition can be expressed many ways, not only with a thank you, but through the appraisal process, through informal chats, through pay increases as appropriate, and occasionally through promotion.

ACTION TODAY

Write down the names of each person reporting directly to you. Then against each name list the three most important things that person has contributed during the last three months. Call each one in turn and informally advise him or her of your assessment. Don't wait for Personnel to send you the appraisal forms next November. Tell each person you value their contribution. Thank them for it. (If you can't identify his or her contribution you have a big problem anyway. You may as well fire the person, or yourself.)

REMEMBER

It takes a SUPERBOSS to recognize managerial excellence.

RELIABILITY

PRODUCT RELIABILITY, PROFIT RELIABILITY, AND SERVICE RELIABILITY REFLECT THE RELIABILITY OF MANAGEMENT.

Reliability, or lack of it, is a reflection of an organization's culture, of its infrastructure, and of the influence its managers have within it.

If you can rely on the Chief Executive to achieve a result, more likely than not you can rely on every single person in the organization to do the same. If you can rely on the Vice President of Marketing to keep his or her word, more likely than not you can rely on every single person in marketing doing the same.

Reliability is a value upon which the Superboss places great store. He prides himself on his own reliability as well as insisting that his people are reliable, too. If the Superboss makes a promise, you can rely on him keeping it. For example, when the Superboss visits an off-base location and informally says he'll look into a problem raised, then you can rely on him looking into that problem and reporting back.

The Superboss stresses to his team the importance of reliability: "I don't want the employee representatives coming in here telling me you haven't installed the drinking fountains you promised for three months ago." He stresses the importance of reliability as far as the customer is concerned: "If you told Colmer's you'd deliver Friday, then I'm afraid you've got no option. You deliver Friday or take the consequences of your lack of reliability."

The Superboss knows that reliability runs alongside accountability as a key element in the successful management of people. The reliability of a Superboss helps establish his credibility and reputation. It helps establish trust and respect. Most importantly, it is the cornerstone of the company's future success, because the risks are minimized when you have a reliable Superboss.

ACTION TODAY

Undertake a "Reliability Analysis." Jot down all recent commitments by yourself and your people. Tick off those where the commitment has been honored. Call up your team and give urgent attention to the balance. Areas of unreliability should be of a serious concern.

ACTION TOMORROW

Analyze any "complaints" you have received, either internally or externally, for lack of reliability in your department over the last twelve months. Prepare a bar chart with, say, 30 red bars for 30 complaints. Keep a twelve-month running total and plot your progress in improving reliability month by month.

REMEMBER

The SUPERBOSS never compromises reliability by accepting or making excuses.

REPORTING RELATIONSHIPS

EVERYONE SHOULD KNOW WHO HIS IMMEDIATE BOSS IS. WITHOUT THAT THERE CAN BE NO AUTHORITY NOR REPORTING RELATIONSHIP.

It might sound obvious, but it is amazing to find that there are companies where some employees do not know who their immediate boss is.

In one company I visited some while back one group of over three hundred people named the same person as their boss. The operations staff, the customer-liaison people, the supervision, and a few others all named the Operations Manager as their boss.

The hard-working supervisors worked different shifts from the operations staff and tended to act as progress chasers and problem solvers for each period of duty. With employees seeing a different supervisor each shift a dangerous supervisory vacuum arose. These people effectively had no permanent boss and this led, over a period of time, to a virtually uncontrollable employee relations situation.

The Superboss places high priority in establishing formal and clear reporting lines throughout his organization, whether it be ten people or ten thousand. He expects to know who his own boss is and he expects every person in his organization to know theirs. The Superboss appreciates that matrix reporting lines are sometimes inevitable, for example where the divisional accountant might report directly to the divisional director and additionally report professionally to the group finance director.

The Superboss will spend a considerable amount of time working at these reporting lines and ensuring they are clear. He knows that for people to perform effectively they must have an immediate boss who sees them regularly, who can recognize their individual contribution, who can give them feedback on how to improve their skills, who can help them address their individual problems, who can encourage them to do better. Also every employee needs an immediate boss to turn to for advice, for decisions and for help.

ACTION TODAY

Examine the organization chart for your section, department, division, or company. (If there isn't an up-to-date one, shame on you. Draw it up immediately.) Cast an eagle eye over it for "funny" reporting lines, lines that go round corners, duck under others, or bypass levels of command. Question any such irregularities. Are they really necessary? Unless you have a very clean organization with clear reporting lines for everyone (which will be the case in good companies with Superbosses) start thinking how you might clear up the mess. Forget about actual people and ensure that each job has a clear-cut reporting line to a higher level job. To help with this clarification process call in your local organization expert, whether he or she be an external consultant, someone from Personnel, or a key member of your team. Spend some days carefully thinking through how you're going to clear up these relationships.

Then consider carefully how you are going to implement any changes.

Don't push this page aside and take it for granted your reporting relationships are clear. The disease is more widespread than most people think.

REMEMBER

You must get your reporting relationships straight to be a SUPERBOSS.

RESILIENCE

WHEN EVERYONE ELSE HAS GIVEN UP, THE RESILIENT MANAGER WILL STILL BE THERE, AND WILL SUCCEED.

It's one of those days! The phone never stops ringing, there's a queue of people at your door with urgent problems, the mail is piling up, you have to be at the sales office two miles down the road within ten minutes, and now, to make matters worse, your boss, Paul Gates, has called you in on some urgent matter.

This is when the Superboss will relax a little, drink a cup of coffee, and do some thinking.

He won't panic; he'll just call in his secretary and calmly give her some instructions: "Ring the sales office please and apologize to them that I'll be along five minutes late. I'm going to leave the mail till this evening unless there's any dynamite there. Now who is it outside? I'll have five seconds with Rebecca Well and sign that urgent travel authorization, but perhaps you'll ask Mick Clarke and Sue Dorsten to come back after lunch. Meanwhile I'd better make that quick phone call to Paul Gates."

The Superboss is resilient. He can take the pressure. He takes it as it comes, constantly reordering his priorities but never letting others down. He is imperturbable, knowing that he is only doing his best. You will never see a Superboss panic, never hear him cry out in despair. You will never hear him yell at people when the pressure's on.

When the pressure is on, the Superboss will take everything in his stride, calmly tackling the priority problems but taking care not to neglect the everyday needs of his people. When the pressure's on, the Superboss doesn't try to do everything himself, he delegates, sometimes waits. When the pressure's on, the Superboss is in control, not out of control, that's how resilient he is.

ACTION TODAY

Find an old Christmas or birthday card. Turn it inside out and write on the blank side: RESILIENCE. WHEN THE PRESSURE'S ON, TAKE TWO MINUTES OFF AND THINK.

Leave that card on your desk so that nobody else can see it. Study it for two minutes next time you really feel you're under pressure.

Then bounce back.

REMEMBER

The SUPERBOSS is so resilient you will never see him torn apart.

RESPECT — MANAGERS WHO DO NOT RESPECT THEIR PEOPLE ARE DICTATORS.

The demonstration of disrespect is one of the most worrying features of many organizations. Management has no respect for the unions. The unions have no respect for management, and demonstrate it vociferously. Sales departments have no respect for personnel, and personnel has no respect for operations. Archie Tolworth, supervisor, has no respect for his, in his view, incompetent boss Dave Smith, and in turn Dave Smith, the Production Manager, has no respect for Clive Manning, the new Operations Director the company has just brought in.

The culture of disrespect, instead of producing profit, produces much finger pointing and back-biting and in the end a loss of confidence in the company, its products, its management, and its people. Disrespect is a dead loss.

You'll recognize a Superboss. Talk to his people. They respect him. Talk to him. He respects his people. He respects the unions he deals with. He respects the fact that each person has a vital contribution to make towards the success of the company. He also respects that each person is an individual with individual needs, problems and inadequacies. He respects that each individual needs help as much as he does.

The Superboss shows respect in the courteous and polite way he treats people and talks to them. He respects that whoever they are they have a viewpoint. He therefore always listens carefully.

The Superboss respects a person for all his or her good points and tries to help him or her overcome the bad points. He respects the trade unions, not because he necessarily agrees with them all the time — he doesn't — but because they are there because his people want them there, and they have an important role to play.

With mutual respect the Superboss treats everyone in the way that he would want to be treated. If a union official shows disrespect, he'll confront the issue with respect. Then he'll forgive and forget.

ACTION TODAY

Be honest! Cast your mind back to your last gossip session (perhaps yesterday at lunch with one or two of your friends). Try to remember who you criticized behind their backs. Perhaps you said to your closest colleague: "I don't know what that crazy Chief Executive is doing, cutting back on travel. He's an idiot! How can I do my job?"

Try to identify the "plus" points of whoever you criticized (behind their backs). There will be many. Discipline yourself to concentrate on these "plus" points next time you speak about that person. Show some respect.

REMEMBER

For whatever you're worth, the SUPERBOSS will respect you.

RESPONSIBILITY

RESPONSIBILITY IS THAT DIFFICULT-TO-DEFINE BURDEN CARRIED ON A MANAGER'S BACK.

There is a distinct difference between responsibility, authority, and accountability. Authority is the power vested in a manager to make specific decisions (for example, on expenditure or recruitment) or to speak on behalf of the company.

Accountability is the requirement for managers to account for the decisions they make and for the successes or failures these decisions lead to.

Responsibility is much broader. To be responsible is to carry a personal burden for everything one controls in one's area and to bear the consequence of the actions under control. The consequence of that action might have an impact on other employees, customers and the community. Responsibility embraces authority and accountability. Responsibility is the total burden and in any management job it is very difficult to define.

If a manager treats an employee harshly and aggressively, and soon after that the employee suffers a breakdown, is the manager responsible?

If a manager tries to save money by contracting with a cheaper but less well-known supplier, and then that supplier goes bust, is the manager responsible for non-delivery?

The mark of a Superboss is that he'll carry responsibility for everything that happens within his area. He won't shrug off responsibility and blame suppliers or an individual's lack of mental fitness. The Superboss feels responsible if his decisions have repercussions in his people's private lives. He feels responsible if he inadvertently lets down his customers, or if he fails to take good advice from one of his people.

For the Superboss responsibility is a matter of conscience. If things go wrong in his area, and they often do, he won't attempt to assign blame for the failure to his boss, nor to the company's poor policies, nor to his people for not understanding. The Superboss will accept the responsibility.

ACTION TODAY

Answer these questions:

Do you feel responsible for your people?

Do you feel responsible for their selection?

Do you feel responsible for their training?

Do you feel responsible for their welfare?

Do you feel responsible for their morale?

Do you feel responsible for the impact of your decisions on their private lives?

Do you feel responsible for their careers?

Do you feel responsible for their pay?

Do you feel responsible for their performance?

Do you feel responsible for what they achieve?

AGAIN: Do you feel responsible for your people?

Should any answer be "No," think very carefully and ask the question again. If you're not responsible for the performance of your people, who is? If you are not responsible for the other factors contributing to performance, who is?

Should each answer be "Yes," think very carefully. Do you really mean it? Do you? Do you feel responsible for your people?

QUESTION

Who is responsible for the SUPERBOSS?

RESULTS | RESULTS ARE THE ONLY MEASURE OF A MANAGER'S PERFORMANCE.

Some managers don't get past stage one. Stage one is to differentiate between the task and the end result. To use a simple example, a bus driver's job is not merely to drive a bus (that's just a task), but to deliver passengers safely and on time from Point A to Point B (the result).

Some managers think that their job is to carry out the task of pushing paper around (for example, signing expenses), to attend committee meetings and mouth comments, to go and have a chat with the gang, or to drink tea with employee representatives. Such managers think that the method of their job (the actual process of doing it) is the job.

The Superboss sees things differently. He sees his job as achieving a distinct business result for the company. In line management jobs, that result might be achieving a sales quota or a production target. In a staff management job, it might be achieving a certain volume of cost-effective training or a target number of new recruits by a given date.

The results a Superboss achieves relate to his objectives. Provided the law is not broken, company policies and procedures not breached, human dignity not impaired, the Superboss is far less interested in the methods his staff use than in the results they achieve. Although the Superboss might help them develop their methods, he won't police them. You won't see, for example, a Superboss looking out of the window at 8:30 each morning counting how many people are arriving late. He won't issue memos telling people to tighten up on punctuality or to use both sides of a sheet of paper. (I have seen it done many a time.)

Essentially the Superboss is results-oriented rather than method-mad. He knows that the means to an end are not an end in themselves. It's easy to kick a football, much more difficult to score a goal.

ACTION TODAY

Concentrate your attention on the results you have to achieve during the next month. Write them down, become preoccupied with their achievement. Each result must be measurable, either qualitatively or quantitatively. While you might examine your own methods of achieving these results, leave your staff to determine their methods. Help them where possible. Avoid imposing methods. "You must do it this way" is bad. "You must achieve this" is better.

REMEMBER

He's the SUPERBOSS because of the results he has achieved.

REVIEWS ALWAYS REVIEW PROGRESS FIRST AND PEOPLE SECONDLY.

Profit through people. People come first. You cannot profit without them.

But when considering the review process, look at the results first, and only then look at the person who's achieved those results.

If you attempt to review the person first you'll soon lose sight of the results. You'll be reviewing Charles Mowdray's behavior. (Is being aggressive a good or bad thing?) You'll be reviewing Jan Francis's ability to communicate. (Is talking too little a good or bad thing?) You'll be reviewing the number of hours put in by George Howard. (Does working long hours lead to better results?) You'll be reviewing the person, but not the results.

The Superboss undertakes periodic progress reviews. He'll bring his team around the table every Monday morning and spend half an hour reviewing what results were achieved last week. Perhaps once a month he might devote half a day for an in-depth review of year-to-date progress against budget.

In addition to team reviews the Superboss carries out periodic reviews with each member of his team, perhaps once a month. He'll review the results Charles Mowdray achieved on the sales front. The trend is downwards and the Superboss will trace this to Charles' sharp edgy behavior. Having reviewed the results, the Superboss will then, if necessary, review the person. Sometimes it's not necessary. Despite Jan Francis's personal problems and her shy retiring manner, she consistently shows she can get the business. He only needs to look at Jan's results. However, there's a problem with George Howard. George always arrives at the office before him and is always there after he leaves. In spite of this he can't seem to produce the accounts on time. The results are unsatisfactory, so the Superboss will review what he can do to help.

ACTION TODAY

You can't know what progress you are making unless you systematically review it. Check your appointment book and ensure that you have regular progress review meetings with your team, and separately with each individual. Discipline yourself to look only at the results to begin with and then, if need be, at the person.

REMEMBER

In reviewing progress a SUPERBOSS is measuring your contribution.

REWARDS — THE WORST FORM OF REWARD IS MONEY.

Pavlov's theory went out of fashion a long time ago. You cannot treat people like dogs. They're more intelligent and will quickly learn how to beat the system by obtaining the reward without giving the desired response.

In the management vocabulary, rewards should be differentiated from incentives. A reward is essentially a form of recognition after the event, while an incentive is an enticement before the event.

Recognition of an employee's contribution is essential and it is important from time to time to reward an exceptional contribution. Although there is nothing intrinsically wrong with giving monetary rewards, it has the danger of corrupting the pay system and de-motivating the very people you want to motivate.

The Superboss maintains a great reservoir of rewards, mostly non-financial. It starts with a smile or a pat on the back. It goes on to be a letter of appreciation or a telephone call and could end up by being a dinner on the company, a bunch of flowers, or a bottle of whiskey. Once a year when something exceptional has happened he might authorize a short overseas company-paid vacation for someone. It will have to be exceptional and the Superboss will be highly discriminating in making the decision. He'll be confident about the precedent and that there will be no pressure to breach it. (If an employee's invention to recycle scrap saved the company half a million, would you begrudge as a reward a short overseas trip paid for by the company?)

When people work for the Superboss they don't aim to receive rewards. The satisfaction of achieving good results is sufficient. They trust their Superboss enough to know that when they put themselves out with some exceptional performance he will reward them. And he will. He'll call them in at the end of a long hard day, pass around the beer and wine, and reward them with a smile and a brief word of thanks.

ACTION TODAY

Initiate your own rewards ceremony. For example, if you run an office convene the ceremony for 4:00 p.m. on the last Friday of next month. Consult your team and brainstorm as many types of rewards as possible. (For example, a reward for the friendliest person on the third floor, for the person who typed the most memos, for the person who stayed on late to take an urgent overseas phone call.) The rewards should be of minimal value (a bar of chocolate, a pen, a bottle of aspirins). You should serve tea, coffee, and biscuits. Make it a fun occasion and then announce that in six months time you'll be giving a reward to the person who devises the most original list of rewards.

If you lead a team of truck drivers, take them out for a Chinese meal next Saturday night and at the end of the dinner make a little speech and reward the laziest driver with a mock parking ticket.

REMEMBER

The SUPERBOSS seeks no reward other than the satisfaction of seeing his people do well.

RULES

RULES SHOULD BE COMMON SENSE. AS A RULE, A MANAGER SHOULD NOT BE A RULER.

Rules exist for the general welfare of every person in the company.

Good companies always have a little booklet listing the rules. "No alcohol on the premises. White hats and coats must be worn in all food preparation areas," and so on.

The great thing about a Superboss is he knows when to break the rules. Only because it's common sense. "Look, Anita", he'll say to his new secretary on her first day, "the rule in this company is that you start at 9, have forty minutes for lunch between noon and 2 and finish at 5:30. Now it's no problem if you want to get in a little late one day, say 9:30, work through your lunch hour or stay a little late. We're prepared to be flexible in this department."

The Superboss will fight for an exception to the rules when he feels it appropriate. He'll go to the travel department and say to the supervisor: "Margo, I know the rules with regard to air travel for supervisory staff, but Arnold Hamilton has volunteered to fly to New York on Friday, work all through Saturday and most of Sunday to get that urgent customer problem fixed and then return Sunday night for that vital engineering review meeting on Monday afternoon. He's sacrificing his whole weekend and I want a first-class ticket for him. If you won't accept my authority for breaking the rules, then you and I have a problem. Let's go upstairs to Dick Tauber's office and get it resolved there."

But when the Superboss is not occasionally breaking the rules, he's ensuring for the rest of the time that people are keeping within them. He won't turn a blind eye if Andy Calver isn't wearing safety shoes, nor if Dickie Bird parks in the visitors' car park when it's raining. Rules are there to be respected and the Superboss ensures they are. Every time they are broken without his authority it undermines that authority and reduces his credibility in the eyes of others.

ACTION TODAY

This is an easy one. Examine your company rules booklet and remind yourself what's in it. Don't go looking for anyone breaking the rules (that's a witch hunt, and is unnecessary). Keep the rules at the back of your mind and take action should you come across an abuse.

If there are no company rules, take the initiative and write them. Send them to Employee Relations, ask them to consult the appropriate people and then issue them.

QUESTION

What rules apply to a SUPERBOSS?

SECURITY

SECURITY OF EMPLOYMENT SHOULD BE SECOND ONLY TO SECURITY OF PROFITS AS A STRATEGIC MANAGEMENT OBJECTIVE.

There is an argument that if you make people too secure in their jobs they'll become complacent, inefficient, take everything for granted, and will not give of their all. But it's an irrelevant argument.

In today's world no employee can be 100 percent secure, because in a competitive environment profit can never be 100 percent secure. A simple fact of life which often escapes employees and their union representatives is that an organization needs revenue, not only to finance wages but also to make profit and give a return to those who have risked their own money to invest in the company. Never forget the shareholders.

The Superboss reminds his people of this when from time to time they get lulled into the illusion that the company is a bottomless reservoir of money. "The best way you can keep your jobs and salaries secure," he will tell them, "is to give of your best."

No company, and therefore no Superboss, can guarantee security of employment. Even so the Superboss will see any attack on his people's jobs as a last resort and to that extent he'll fight to protect them. For example, if there has to be a choice between cutting marketing costs or jobs, he'll cut marketing costs, even if he has to slash his huge but precious advertising budget. He wants his staff to be secure in the knowledge that pay and jobs, in that order, will always be the last to be cut.

The Superboss also attempts to provide security on a day-by-day basis. He doesn't want others to feel insecure because they don't know what's going on, or don't know what he's thinking of them. He doesn't want them to be suspicious about arbitrary decisions being made behind their backs. The Superboss therefore believes that straight talking and honest communication are essential for minimizing any feelings of insecurity employees might have. He knows that people work best when they feel secure; that if they feel insecure they will worry, fret, and waste time huddling in corners chatting. The Superboss therefore attempts to make their jobs and pay secure, but without being able to guarantee it.

ACTION TODAY

Do you know how secure your people feel with respect to you and the company? First, ask how secure you feel yourself. Should you feel insecure, then address that issue today. Discuss it with your boss, get the facts and work hard to minimize the insecurity, for yourself and for your people.

But never offer guarantees.

REMEMBER

A SUPERBOSS and his team are only as secure as the profitable performance of the company allows.

| **SELECTION** | WHEN YOU SELECT THE PERSON, YOU SELECT A POTENTIAL CONTRIBUTION TO PROFIT. |

It starts here. The selection process is vital to the future success of any company.

You would have thought that was glaringly obvious, but I've seen many companies where managers fail to give sufficient time to this critical task (ask any recruitment specialist).

Such managers will change interview dates four times in four weeks, or cram a fifteen-minute interview between two other meetings and then spend the whole interview doing the talking themselves. They'll refuse to give any time to the essential task of discussing with Recruitment the main requirements for the job and the ideal candidate they're looking for. They'll finally select someone with blue eyes.

I remember once an interviewer calling me by a wrong name. He had the papers of another candidate in front of him.

The Superboss gives the highest priority to selecting the best person for the job. He'll spend a considerable amount of time on it and involve many others to get additional opinions. Where appropriate he'll use selection techniques such as psychometric testing and assessment centers. At the interview he'll allow the candidate to do most of the talking (although he will need to persuade the candidate that it's a company worth joining, and that he's a Superboss to work for). The Superboss will ensure other people interview the shortlist candidates and he'll value their judgment, especially if someone raises doubts about his preferred choice.

Although the Superboss will do his best to ensure the selected candidate meets the required specification, he'll occasionally take a risk. He'll use his intuition and, on the basis of the candidate's personality, attitude, and potential, select someone who doesn't have all the required experience. In the case of selection, skill and potential are often more important than experience.

The Superboss never allows subjective considerations or prejudice to influence his selection decisions. He works within the law, does not countenance discrimination, and will objectively select the best person.

ACTION TODAY

Ask your recruitment specialist to set up a formal review meeting on selection methods in your department. The objective will be to improve them. It is vital that you always select the best person for the job, and that requires time.

At the review critically examine how much time you invest in the selection of any one individual. Unless you're a Superboss you'll probably find it's insufficient and you are making rushed choices. (The average selection will take about ten hours of the Superboss's time.)

REMEMBER

A SUPERBOSS is among the select in management.

SOUNDING BOARD

A SOUNDING BOARD IS AN INSTRUMENT FOR TURNING ORGANIZATION NOISE INTO HARMONIC PROGRESS.

We all need someone to talk with informally and confidentially; someone off whom we can bounce ideas, with whom we can let off steam, to whom we can moan and groan. No person can be an island.

Managers are no different. They need someone at work to turn to in total confidence for a second opinion, to test out crazy ideas, or with whom to relax for three to thirty minutes.

The Superboss has one or two close colleagues whom he uses as a sounding board. He might pop in to see them for a quick cup of coffee first thing in the morning, or just before going home. He'll have a chat, ask for their opinions on things going on.

But the Superboss has other sounding boards, too. He will be constantly sounding out people in his area about important issues. At the end of his weekly team briefing he might say, "Just before we close, I'd welcome your views about this new job evaluation system that employee relations are proposing."

When he walks around and chats with the cleaners last thing at night, he'll sound them out on what they think of the proposed new layout. The Superboss will also use his own boss as a sounding board, taking him into his confidence about important changes he is planning.

He also encourages other people to use him as a sounding board—his junior staff to sound out new ideas on him, or his immediate subordinates to sound him out on solving problems. The Superboss will always lend a sympathetic, understanding ear.

ACTION TODAY

Ask your secretary to set up a series of monthly one-hour "sounding board sessions." Anyone in your area can attend (first come, first served, maximum 20). At each meeting everyone is free to raise issues, ideas, or problems which they want to sound out in the group and also with the boss.

As you've initiated the session you perhaps should start the ball rolling by sounding out the group on a couple of ideas you have. Leave plenty of time for them to sound you out on other issues.

REMEMBER

If you have a SUPERBOSS, you will already be on his sounding board.

STANDARDS — EVERY MANAGER NEEDS STANDARDS.

Nobody would deny that you cannot manage without standards. The problem is that in many companies standards are not very well defined and, what is worse, not applied. Just look at the difference in service standards between a good restaurant and a poor one. The difference is one of management standards. The same applies to airlines. Most people can tell you a hundred "war stories" about varying standards in airlines.

It's not only service standards, but also standards of report writing, of presentation, of dress, of behavior, and many others.

The Superboss sees the definition and maintenance of standards as a key management task. The standards he sets are crystal clear, are understood by everyone in his division and, equally importantly, accepted as being necessary. Let's take, for example, standards of dress. These days the Superboss will recognize that people require a high degree of creative freedom in deciding how to dress. He will therefore develop a standard which gives scope for this (though he would not allow dress which outrages customers, the visitors, or the immediate team). Cliff French's green hair might just be acceptable, while Val Sanders' cool braless attire with a see-through blouse might not!

But it's not only dress. The Superboss will set standards for the recruitment people relating to the efficiency of their response to unsolicited applications. He'll set standards of housekeeping in the canteen. He'll set standards of appearance for company vehicles. He'll set standards for supervisory training, for performance appraisal, and for written communications.

Having set the standards, having got them understood and accepted, he'll establish controls to ensure they are maintained. Nothing reduces the credibility of a manager more than when he or she sets a standard and then doesn't attempt to maintain it.

ACTION TODAY

Arrange for an item "standards" to be put on the agenda of your next team meeting. At that meeting review with your team what they consider to be the main standards of performance and behavior in your division. Before the meeting do some careful preparation so that you, as leader of the team, can spell out what you consider to be the most important standards. Make sure that your team agrees on the control procedures and that these are followed.

ACTION NEXT MONTH

At your team meeting, review whether or not these standards have been achieved.

REMEMBER

The SUPERBOSS sets the highest possible standards and consistently maintains them.

STYLE — TO ACHIEVE DISTINCTION IN MANAGEMENT YOU NEED STYLE.

Style is a mark of distinction. Style differentiates one company's approach to management from another. It differentiates the good manager from the bad. Style is the distinctive way in which a manager behaves, in which he or she appears, in which he or she expresses him or herself.

Excellent companies set out to develop a distinguished style of management, one which they know will optimize their chances of success and with which excellent managers will readily identify.

The Superboss favors a style of management which is open and honest, is both results- and people-oriented, is communicative, co-operative, and decisive. It is a hard-working, positive and constructive style of management with an equal concern for the company and its people.

The Superboss has developed his style over a number of years. He still thinks carefully about it and always tries to behave consistently. Furthermore, although he allows his supervisors and managers to develop their own personal styles, he encourages them to align those styles as closely as possible with his own and that of the company. If the Superboss has a warm outgoing style, then he won't insist that a quiet and slightly reserved supervisor changes to the same. However, he will encourage that supervisor to develop a style based on trust and mutual respect, on sincerity and integrity, a style compatible with that of the Superboss and his team.

While the Superboss does not want each of his team to be personality clones of himself, he does want them to develop a distinctive, professional, and positive style which they can all identify with and feel confident in.

Absence of identifiable style leads to concern about unpredictable behavior and arbitrariness. People want their leader to have a well-defined style because they will then know where they stand with him.

ACTION TODAY

Call in a consultant or your closest confidant at work and ask him or her to describe honestly your style of management. Does the description accord with your own view? Discuss it, evaluate it, and then look for opportunities of improving your style. Perhaps you come across as a waffler, a ditherer, a procrastinator or as being indecisive, always passing the buck. Ask yourself why another manager along the road appears to be positively the opposite. Perhaps you can learn by observing that manager's style and that of other successful managers.

REMEMBER

You can distinguish a SUPERBOSS by his style.

| SUPPORT | WHEN THE COMPANY SUPPORTS ITS EMPLOYEES, ITS EMPLOYEES WILL SUPPORT THE COMPANY. |

The analogy of seeing people as costs or assets is critical here.

Costs are things to be attacked, reduced, and minimized. Costs are a necessary evil that detract from profit. Costs are things against which blunt axes are wielded when there's a downturn in profit. Costs are not to be supported.

Assets are the things you invest in and the substance from which profit is derived. Assets have to be protected, maintained, and developed. They are the heart of the business. Assets have to be supported.

The Superboss sees his people as assets in the organization. Their support for the company is an asset. He knows that he cannot achieve their support unless he supports them with good pay, good training, good working conditions, good tools, good back-up services, and good leadership. They will be aware of his genuine support.

However, his support is not only tangible in terms of pay and working conditions. He gives them moral support, too. He has their interests at heart and will support them in the pursuit of these interests (albeit not at the expense of the company; they are the company). He'll support them in getting problems fixed; he'll support them in any profit-making improvements they want to make. His support shows and they appreciate it and reciprocate.

The Superboss will also support every individual in his area (whether he or she be one of 10, 100, or 1,000). He'll support and protect that individual's rights as an employee. He'll support any fair cause that has to be fought on behalf of that employee. He'll give moral support when problems arise, when help is needed. He'll lend support with encouragement, warmth, and advice whenever it's required.

ACTION TODAY

By hook or by crook find an opportunity of offering support to at least three people today.

To do so forget about yourself completely and put yourself in the shoes of whomever you meet. Discuss problem areas, opportunity areas, and see if you can identify a way of supporting them to solve their problems, exploiting their opportunities.

Set yourself the objective of developing a reputation as a supportive manager.

REMEMBER

The SUPERBOSS genuinely supports his people all the time, not just when he wants something.

SYSTEMS — THERE IS NO SYSTEM THAT CAN BE SUBSTITUTED FOR MANAGING PEOPLE SUCCESSFULLY.

You might have thought that personnel systems were actually taking over the process of managing people. All you had to do was fill in the forms, the appraisal forms, the MBO worksheets, the climate surveys, the assessment center tests, the psychometric tests, the succession plans, the training needs analyses, the career review forms, the briefing sheets and, finally, the termination reports.

Well here's a breath of fresh air. The Superboss doesn't need all that nonsense. Or, to be more accurate, he doesn't need all those systems and all the paper they produce.

But don't delude yourself. The Superboss knows that underneath all that unnecessary paperwork are some essential principles of management.

The Superboss might not need an appraisal form, but he'll give the highest priority to appraising his people. Appraisal forms were invented by Personnel to force incompetent managers to appraise their staff. The incompetent managers filled in the forms and remained incompetent. Personnel thought they had done a good job, but their contribution to profit was negative. They actually increased the cost of administering incompetent managers.

The Superboss sets objectives, but doesn't need forms to do it. In fact he considers setting objectives essential to his management task, as he does assessing the climate or mood of his people and their capability; not to mention, of course, the essential need to identify training requirements, to review careers, and to brief his people.

The Superboss uses paper sparingly to support these essential tasks of management. He's not even against a simple system as long as it is sensible, efficient, and actually helps with the job.

There's nothing wrong with an appraisal form if you find it helpful. I personally prefer blank sheets of paper.

ACTION TODAY

Don't let this section incite you to rebellion against all the personnel systems in the company. The last thing you should do is photocopy these two pages and wave them in the face of the Personnel Manager when he or she reminds you that you are two months behind with your appraisal schedule.

Be more positive. Do the appraisals. The form filling is the least important aspect.

Look at all the other personnel systems and rather than complain about the bureaucracy just ask yourself why someone thinks they're necessary. It could be that you're not doing too good a job managing your people.

REMEMBER

The system is there to help the SUPERBOSS.

TALENT — ONE OF THE MOST EXCITING MANAGEMENT TASKS IS TALENT SPOTTING.

You don't spot talent by filling in and reading appraisal forms, nor by going to Personnel and ploughing through 200 centrally-filed career potential review reports.

You don't spot talent by sitting on committees, nor by doing the work of your subordinates.

The Superboss spots talent because he notices when Lindsey Brown gives a superb presentation, or when Dan Shutze does an excellent supervisory job in an emergency, or because several customers tell him, "That Lyn Zaleski is the best salesperson you've put in our department for a long while. She really knows what she's talking about. She knows your catalogue, she's service-oriented, always delivers, always keeps her word and, what's more, in her quiet efficient way is superb at handling the obnoxious bastards in our office."

The Superboss keeps an eye out for talent and excellence all the time. When he reads Rob Smith's Stage 3 report the Superboss will tell himself that this guy really knows how to put together a clear, succinct, well presented report. He knows that he's done his homework, presented the facts well, and that his recommendations are soundly based. The Superboss will have spotted a talent.

The Superboss will create opportunities for others to show their talents. He'll organize presentations so that up-and-coming people can speak about their achievements, their plans, their work. The Superboss will walk the shop floor with half an eye out for potential supervisors. For the Superboss, talent spotting is one of his most enjoyable pursuits at work.

ACTION TODAY

Here's some bureaucracy. Take a blank sheet of paper and write down the names of the most talented people in your department. These should be juniors who do not directly report to you.

Now write down the reasons you believe these people are so talented. Ask your immediate team to give you their list. Compare the names and then discuss the reasons for any lack of overlap.

FUTURE ACTION

Do the same thing in six months' time and compare notes. In a year's time pull out the notes and establish how many of these talented people have been promoted out of your department. If the answer is zero you have failed to spot and develop talent.

Now, today, go back a year and do the same thing retrospectively. What talent have you spotted and developed during these last twelve months?

REMEMBER

The SUPERBOSS has an eye for talent and develops it.

TEAMS IF A MANAGER DOESN'T HAVE A TEAM, HE OR SHE CAN'T BE A MANAGER.

To be a team you have to work together.

In one company I knew, the top team was a group of individuals rather than individuals in a group. Each did his own individual thing, giving less than enthusiastic support to company decisions while pursuing selfish sectional interests enthusiastically. The lack of cohesiveness in the top team was perceived throughout the company and had an alarmingly negative impact on the management climate.

The Superboss carefully builds his team. He chooses people who he knows are going to work well together, who are going to support each other, who are all going to identify with the cause. Within the team the various members will use their own strengths to balance each other's weaknesses. Each member will have the opportunity to have his or her say when it comes to important decisions.

The Superboss cares for his team and spends considerable time with them. He'll brief them regularly, once a day, once a week, or once a month, depending on logistics and the actual business. He'll hold regular consultative meetings at which any team member can raise an agenda item.

He'll hold informal lunchtime sessions when they can chew the cud and air any topic they wish. Once or twice a year the Superboss will take his team away for a day or two, not only for an in-depth look at progress and future plans, but for some team building around the bars.

The Superboss expects and receives complete loyalty from the team. Any individual can say his or her piece before a decision is made, but once that decision is made the Superboss expects full commitment to it. He will not tolerate anybody working against the team and would treat such "de-commitment" by a team member as a resignation issue.

For the Superboss the team is all.

ACTION TODAY

Consult two people. First your management development special-ist or a consultant. Then your boss. How do they see your team functioning? Do they see it working well together? Do they see much backbiting, moaning, and groaning? In their opinion is there a need for further team building? Listen carefully to what they say and compare it with your own perceptions.

ACTION NEXT WEEK

Feed back to your team the various views about how you work together, and discuss this with them. Agree on ways of further developing the cohesiveness of the team.

REMEMBER

The SUPERBOSS never forgets that he is not only leader of the team, but part of it.

THANKS | IT'S SO HARD TO PLEASE WHEN YOU RECEIVE NO THANKS.

The Superboss thanks his secretary for getting in early.

The Superboss thanks his boss for giving him that tip-off about Mathieson's.

The Superboss thanks Tony Adcock for cleaning out the sludge tank last night.

The Superboss thanks Gabriel Ramirez for raising that issue about the leaky roof.

The Superboss writes an individual note of thanks to each of the three engineers who went out in gale-force conditions over the weekend to recover that heavy goods vehicle that broke down.

The Superboss writes a note of thanks to the employee relations specialist who had to deal with some distraught parents when one of the company's apprentices was killed in a motorcycle accident.

The Superboss rings Sydney Owens to thank him for a superb lunch.

The Superboss writes a note of thanks to the security man who went out of his way to get his car started for him.

The Superboss thanks Michele Roberts for staying late to send off some urgent mail.

The Superboss always goes out of his way to thank people and to look for opportunities to show his appreciation. People want the recognition of having done that little extra for a Superboss. They want to be thanked. The process of thanking creates a "giving" rather than a "taking" society where "demands" are the order of the day.

ACTION TODAY

It is so easy to forget to thank, or not to be bothered. Thanking is not a sign of weakness. Go and give some thanks today. If you have nothing to be thankful about, then there is something seriously wrong with your department and especially you.

Starting today, pick up the phone and just say "thanks" to anyone who put themselves out for you.

Starting today, discipline yourself to write at least one thank-you note per week to someone who has put in some extra effort on your behalf and the company.

If you see nothing to thank anyone for, you must go and look for it. If you don't systematically thank people, they will systematically think you are taking them for granted. The consequences should be obvious.

REMEMBER

The SUPERBOSS expects no thanks.

TOLERATION

TOLERATION IS THE ABILITY TO ABSORB FRUSTRATION, THE SUPPLY OF WHICH INCREASES WITH THE SIZE OF THE MANAGEMENT CHALLENGE.

Organizations are full of noise — people who make mistakes, who gossip, who say silly things to the boss, who act strangely. Organizations are even full of people who disagree with the boss.

The Superboss tolerates all this and much more. He absorbs a whole range of frustrations and only takes action when performance is threatened. He tolerates the eccentricities of Ossie Brett, the green-haired punk, but not when he throws a tool in the sludge tank.

He tolerates the people who confront and disagree with him, knowing full well they could be right, even if he doesn't see it that way immediately. The Superboss tolerates the frustrations of the rumor mill, the grapevine, the gossip machines, the scandal-mongers, and the "five-second experts." He knows that he is better off concentrating on scoring goals rather than shouting back at the crowd.

He tolerates the subordinate who humbly admits his mistake, knowing that he or she will learn from that mistake. However, the Superboss will take action when he knows the subordinate has not learned and keeps making the same mistake. The Superboss will not tolerate adverse performance through repetitive mistakes.

ACTION TODAY

Before you go to bed tonight get hold of a large jar. Take it to work and label it "Toleration Jar."

Every time you suffer a silly frustration (your boss flicking dandruff off his collar, or the Finance Director sending you yet another instruction to economize on paper clips) make a note of it. At the end of the day, collect the notes, screw them up, and throw them in the "toleration jar."

Take no further action unless your department's performance is clearly going to be affected.

At the end of the year throw a party for your staff. Unscramble the notes and use these as the basis for your speech. (Don't drink too much beforehand and don't be too personal.) Then ceremonially burn the notes without setting the company on fire.

REMEMBER

It doesn't take much to tolerate a SUPERBOSS.

THE NEW A-Z OF MANAGING PEOPLE

TRAINING — YOU CANNOT TRAIN A MANAGER.

Managers train themselves. Without that motivation for self improvement any attempt to train a manager will be futile.

Training courses are excellent for providing resources, knowledge, wisdom, feedback, and stimulus for managers to improve themselves. But no matter how good the course or how good the instructor, a training course will do nothing for a manager unless he or she has already embarked on a life-long self-training program.

I react sharply, therefore, to managers who complain that the company hasn't trained them. The company might well be at fault for not providing the facilities, for not encouraging training. Such companies are likely to end up with these negative moaners who complain about lack of training. The real answer is to get yourself trained. There is ample opportunity through self-study and self-improvement.

The Superboss encourages his supervision and managers to be trained in the essential skills of leadership, management, and dealing with people. The Superboss doesn't select anyone into his supervisory or managerial team who doesn't want to improve his or her skills in this area. The Superboss will stimulate the debate on managerial excellence and will encourage his team to seize every opportunity to improve. He'll search out the very best training courses and seminars for his people. He'll even call in the company training manager and design his own supervisory and management training program to facilitate the pursuit of managerial excellence.

As far as the Superboss himself is concerned, he will have jumped at any opportunities to improve his own management skills. If he sees a suitable course for himself, he'll ask his boss to put him on it, if his boss hasn't thought about it first. The Superboss will seek out the best management literature to stimulate his thinking on how to improve. He'll often get together with individuals or small groups to talk "management" and to identify ways of improving. He'll encourage feedback about his own management skills so that he can learn from that.

ACTION TODAY

Call in your training manager and undertake a brief review of the training needs of the supervisors and managers in your area. Having identified the needs, ask yourself how motivated each person is to improve.

ACTION TOMORROW

Speak to each person and discuss with him or her the needs you have identified and how motivated he or she is to improve. Once agreed, fix the training.

ACTION NEXT YEAR

Review the success of the training.

REMEMBER

It takes a great amount of self-training to become a SUPERBOSS.

TRAVEL YOU HAVE TO GO A LONG WAY TO SURPASS "TRAVEL" AS A MOTIVATING AGENT.

I had great difficulty writing this section. I dedicated seven whole days in Rio de Janeiro to it and towards the end I seemed more concerned about whether my ever-deepening suntan would survive an overnight flight to London, than whether I'd ever write about travel.

As I sat by the pool under the blazing Brazilian sun and watched the bronzed señoritas sipping their *caiparinhas* I began to wonder why travel was such a motivator. I wandered towards the palm trees on the terrace of the Rio Palace Hotel and gazed down at the hot white sands of the Copacabana Beach curving away towards the *Pao de Acucar* (Sugar Loaf) in the distance.

It was November and I knew that back in my cold dreary homeland millions of people would give anything to be in my place.

Mind you, there would be another million miserable souls who travel a lot, say they hate it, and still do as much as they can.

The Superboss knows that, for the rising junior, international travel is a great motivator. First and foremost it makes him or her feel important, it gives confidence, broadens the mind, and adds excitement to a job.

The Superboss goes out of his way to create travel opportunities for his up-and-coming people. He sends them on courses in Geneva, liaison trips to Mexico City, or research projects to Hong Kong. If a person has done an exceptionally great job (mark the word "exception" — it is not the rule), he'll even send them to Rio de Janeiro and charge it to the company.

The motivational impact of one's first professional international travel is always great. The Superboss will use it selectively and with a high degree of discrimination. Some might say the travel is a "perk," but the Superboss knows that up in the Ivory Tower there are very important people who fly Concorde to New York, reserve hotel suites with Jacuzzis and have meetings around the swimming pool. They call it work, but there's nothing wrong with the occasional "perk" either.

ACTION TODAY

Look at your travel appointment book for the next three months. Invite your most promising people to undertake each travel assignment on your behalf, the exception being if the destination is absolutely terrible. (I daren't suggest any — I've always loved Lagos and San Paulo.)

If you don't travel, and none of your team does, use your imagination and create an opportunity. Don't they produce paper clips more efficiently in Brazil?

REMEMBER

You have to travel a long way to become a SUPERBOSS.

TRUST — TRUST IS THE CORNERSTONE OF ALL MEANINGFUL RELATIONSHIPS, WHETHER AT THE WORKPLACE OR ELSEWHERE.

The issue of trust is one of the most serious for a manager. The Superboss will always have implicit trust in his team, and his team in him.

Without trust no manager can achieve good results. In a climate of distrust organization politics are rife, much energy is expounded protecting backs or kicking others behind theirs. Criticizing everyone but yourself or the person you're talking to is an everyday occurrence. Distrust is blatantly counter-productive. The worst industrial relationships are generated from distrust, often derived from deep-rooted prejudices not founded at all on fact. Distrust often thrives when the reputation, the perception of the person (manager, vice-president, union leader) is far removed from the reality.

The Superboss develops trust by devoting an immense amount of time to building honest relationships with his people. He believes in them, shows it, and subsequently demonstrates that they can believe in him, trust him.

He means what he says and says what he means. The Superboss demonstrates that he is more concerned with fine action than fine words. The Superboss practices what he preaches. He develops trust by encouraging his people, rather than threatening them. If he does have to make a rare threat, then he's prepared to carry it out. He never cries "wolf" — unless there is a wolf.

Absolute honesty, integrity, sincerity, and compassion are the cornerstones on which the Superboss develops trust. He always gives others the benefit of the doubt, never believes bad of them unless they clearly provide evidence of it. He bears neither malice nor grudges because he believes in his people, trusts them to do their very best for him and the company, as he would for them.

ACTION TODAY

Ask yourself about each member of your team. Do you completely trust him or her? If not, face the facts. Take that person aside and confront the issue. Explain why you don't think you trust him or her and then sincerely discuss ways of developing that trust.

Your second action is to find a way of surveying your team and establishing whether they trust you. Perhaps your personnel manager or a consultant could help. Explain to your team why it is so important to know and then agree with them the best way of obtaining the feedback. Don't rush at it. If there is distrust you'll make it worse by embarrassing people into saying things they don't want to say. An anonymous survey by Personnel might be the best way. But you need to follow through.

REMEMBER

You can always trust a SUPERBOSS.

UNDERSTANDING THE PERSON

PUT YOURSELF IN THE OTHER PERSON'S SHOES, THEN YOU'LL UNDERSTAND.

The Superboss always starts from where the other person is.

The Superboss always puts himself in the other person's shoes.

The Superboss always asks himself, "How would I feel if I was this person? What would I be thinking, what expectations would I have from this meeting, what anxieties might there be?"

The problems of the organization are the problems of the people. The Superboss knows he needs to understand the people to understand these problems. He knows that the real problems are often not what people say they are. The Superboss knows that when Stuart Finch says, "The company should really do something about our stinking restroom," he really means, "Our supervisor has done nothing to sort out the problem."

The Superboss understands that others frequently project problems onto "the company" when the resolution lies much closer to home. The Superboss therefore tries very hard to find out what they mean when they say something. He learns to understand what motivates his people, what annoys them, what important problems they're reluctant to talk about. He learns to understand his people.

In trying to understand, the Superboss will learn where the problems really lie. He will learn from the things that remain unsaid, from a certain tension in the air, or a sharp exchange between two people. He'll understand that some people feel inadequate in various aspects of their work, although they'll never admit it to him. Maybe they will be reluctant to submit reports (they are inadequate at writing reports) or lead union meetings (they are frightened of union people). Perhaps they never go to the milling bay (they can't stand the noise).

The Superboss learns to understand his people and their problems, and because he understands he is able to help them and that helps the company.

ACTION TODAY

Think about your people. Put yourself into the shoes of the first five people you meet today. Imagine what they're really thinking, what their problems really are. And then, gently, unassumingly encourage them to talk about these problems. Try to understand; you'll probably learn a lot.

REMEMBER

It's easy to understand why he is a SUPERBOSS.

UNIONS — MANAGEMENT GETS THE UNIONS IT DESERVES.

The subject of unions is more emotional and controversial than the subject of management — at least among management.

There is nothing wrong with unions, except the way they behave sometimes. And the way management behaves towards them.

Unions are there for a purpose. The majority of people want them there. They want them to represent independently their interests and views. There's nothing wrong with that in a democratic society.

The Superboss recognizes this. He encourages responsible union activity. He respects union representatives and officials, takes them into his confidence, seeks their advice. He respects their views even when he disagrees with them.

However, the Superboss doesn't tolerate irresponsible union behavior (nor irresponsible management behavior), for example, breaking procedures or agreements. He doesn't tolerate militant rhetoric, continuous fault finding, back-biting, trouble stirring or gladiatorial slandering matches (whether or not it comes from militant unionists or hard-headed supervisors). Nor does the Superboss tolerate employee relations departments doing deals for his people behind his back. Employee relations specialists (sometimes horse traders, poker players, jungle fighters, wheeler dealers, organization terrorists) can be just as bad as militant unionists (sometimes horse traders, poker players, jungle fighters, wheeler dealers, organization terrorists).

The Superboss involves himself in employee relations and works closely with the specialists as well as the union representatives. He never attempts to fight the unions, but always tries to work with them. If unions are not wanted, then that's not the decision of the Superboss, nor the company. It's the decision of his people.

ACTION TODAY

If there are no unions in your company take the day off, or turn to another section in this book (choose a page number). Or, better still, ask why there are no unions in your company. If there are unions in your company go and wash your brain with a bar of soap and remove all prejudice. Then clench your fist until the whites of the knuckle show and say, "I am determined to work with the union." Repeat this continually until you mean it. Go and work with the union, no matter how difficult it is. That's your management challenge.

QUESTION

Who best represents the interests of employees, the SUPERBOSS or responsible trade unions?

VACATIONS — EXECUTIVES WHO DON'T TAKE THEIR VACATIONS SHOULD BE JAILED FOR TWO WEEKS.

Vacations are essential. No one can do without them.

Vacations have a thousand therapeutic qualities not the least of which is the effect on others when you're away. Vacations present a great opportunity for others to do your job, and even show they can do it better. (Can you believe that's possible?) Vacations give your secretary a chance to catch up on all that paperwork you've left behind. Vacations enable you to prove to yourself that you are not totally indispensable. That's always a salutary lesson.

The Superboss always takes his vacations, not necessarily because he wants to, but because he knows that if he doesn't his team will feel guilty when they take theirs. So the Superboss sets the example and insists that his people follow.

The Superboss actually wants his vacation. He wants the therapy of letting some fresh air flow through his mind. He wants to sit on top of a mountain and take a long cool look at his job and work. He wants to do a little swimming and dive deeply under the surface of what's been happening these last few months. Then after the first two or three days' vacation he wants to forget all about work. He wants to spend some time with his family who he's probably neglected these last few months.

Then, inevitably, when he begins to be bored with his week or two of vacation, he wants to get back to work, invigorated, refreshed with (God help his people!) a thousand new ideas.

ACTION TODAY

This is the best page in the book! Take out your appointment book and plan your next vacation (if it's not planned already). Make sure it happens. No excuses. You must take it. No interruptions during the vacation either, unless the company's going out of business.

Next, and this should be even better, check with your immediate subordinates and make sure they have made their vacation plans. Don't all go at once. Someone might become suspicious.

REMEMBER
Vacations are a great asset to the SUPERBOSS.

VALUE YOUR PEOPLE

NO COMPANY IS WORTH ANYTHING WITHOUT ITS PEOPLE. VALUE THEM.

Don't underestimate your people. They are a priceless part of your organization. They are your company's most important asset. The company could not function if you fired them all tomorrow, nor could you replace them overnight.

The Superboss values his people. While he will try to provide them with a fair and realistic level of pay he knows that you cannot price people this way. He knows that their value lies in their skills, experience, and knowledge, as well as their dedication, commitment, and effort. Their value is reflected in the time and effort he puts into selecting them, developing and sustaining their motivation. (Some managers spend more time choosing their car and caring for it than choosing their people and caring for them.)

Furthermore, the Superboss values his people for what they are. He values their individuality, their unique contribution, the way they work together as a team. He values their opinions and views on what is going on. He values their advice, their understanding, their commitment, and loyalty. He values the sacrifices they make occasionally.

The Superboss never sees his people as a simple cost on the profit and loss account. That is too simplistic a view which treats them as a disposable commodity. (Let's cut down costs. Let's cut down on people.)

The Superboss sees his people as the company's most valuable asset and this is reflected in the time and effort he devotes to protecting and developing that asset.

ACTION TODAY

Undertake a zero base analysis. Assume your immediate team all resign and leave tomorrow. Assess the time it would take to replace them and develop the new appointees to the same performance level as those who left.

Now assume all your people (10, 100, or 1,000) leave tomorrow. Again assess the time it would take to replace them and, furthermore, what the prospects for doing so actually are.

The conclusion should be obvious. Any one person leaving the company is a wasted asset; a waste of all the money, time, and effort you and the company should have invested in that person. Value that investment, value your people.

REMEMBER

A SUPERBOSS is invaluable to your company.

 IT REALLY IS AN IMPOSITION WHEN PEOPLE DON'T VOLUNTEER TO HELP.

If you work in a medium-to-large organization you must have seen those managers who refuse to help with anything. They throw up obstacles against any suggestion, any new approach, any additional effort. They insist on strict demarcation lines, on the rule book being followed to the letter, on procedures never being flexed. They are the managers who never put themselves out.

Nobody ever volunteers to help these negative managers, because they don't even volunteer to help themselves.

If he sees a problem, the Superboss will volunteer to help. If his boss wants a volunteer to represent the company at a conference on the first Saturday in June, the Superboss will volunteer.

The cynics will say that he's naive and being exploited because he is always volunteering to do more than is required of him.

The Superboss doesn't see it that way. He wants to create a climate among his people where they are prepared to volunteer to help each other. The only way he can do this is set the example himself. If the sales team is short of people for a promotional event, the Superboss will volunteer to assist. If his team is struggling with the year-end accounts, the Superboss will volunteer to help. If a graduate trainee is encountering problems with a research project, the Superboss will volunteer some advice.

In volunteering the Superboss never attempts to do other people's jobs. All he is attempting is to provide some additional effort and advice when it is required. By setting that example the Superboss knows that others will follow.

Volunteering to help is being bothered, is putting yourself out. It is recognizing that no person is an island, no person is without need of others.

ACTION TODAY

Go out of your way to volunteer to help someone in your organization, whether it be your boss, your colleagues, or one of your staff. Don't wait to be asked, just volunteer. "Can I give you a hand with that trolley, Sue? Do you want me to telephone Colin Avery on your behalf? I know him quite well."

Starting today, be one step ahead. Volunteer to help; it's much better than being asked.

REMEMBER

The SUPERBOSS always volunteers to help and never ends up helpless.

WALKING ABOUT

WALKING ABOUT IS FAR PREFERABLE TO TALKING IN THE IVORY TOWER WHICH, UNFORTUNATELY, MANY EMPLOYEES THINK THEIR MANAGERS DO MOST OF THE TIME.

The invisible manager is an impossible manager. How can he see what's going on? By reading reports?

The Superboss puts the highest priority on getting out and about, walking, talking, listening, learning, and finding out about his people. He wanders around and finds out what they want to know, what problems they want fixed, what they enjoy about their work (he might even be able to make it more enjoyable). The Superboss shows an interest, shows he cares, shows that he wants his people to do well. He spends five minutes here and five minutes there explaining what's going on in the company while they explain to him what's happening on the job.

This cannot be achieved by issuing memos from the ivory tower, by using suggestion schemes, or producing expensive videos, or sending everyone on brainwashing courses. The Superboss knows it can only be achieved by walking about.

The Superboss also encourages other people to walk about, to give him feedback. They might see things from a different perspective. He wants to learn from everyone. A visible manager is a human manager.

A visible manager walking about is a Superboss facing up to the everyday problems of his team. You may think that your biggest problem is next year's budget, but Colin Carey might be more concerned about his worn out lathe, or why the company cut down on apprentice recruitment this year and his son couldn't even get an interview. The Superboss needs to know, because he knows it will effect his team's motivation and performance.

besides, the Superboss knows that walking about is excellent exercise!

ACTION TODAY

Set yourself a minimum standard of walking around your department at least four times a week. Your secretary should blank out half an hour or more for each of these "walkabouts." They should become routine, but with irregular routes, irregular times, and of varying duration (half an hour to four hours). Take note of any problems you encounter and actions you should take. Don't go behind the supervisor's back. Take him into your confidence, and obtain his cooperation. If you have more than one location, make different plans, but the principle is the same.

ACTION TOMORROW

Ask your employee relations specialist to spend a couple of hours wandering around separately, chatting to people. Then sit down with him or her and review what he or she has found. You'll learn a lot.

ACTION NEXT MONTH

Invite the Chief Executive to walk round your area with you. Introduce him or her to as many of your team as possible. Encourage them to say what they like. Demonstrate to the Chief Executive and your people that you're proud of them.

REMEMBER

You shouldn't have to walk far to see the SUPERBOSS!

THE ABILITY TO WRITE IS AS ELUSIVE AS THE ABILITY TO MANAGE.

One of the distressing things about modern education is that students do not learn to write effectively.

The rudiments of grammar and spelling are hardly sufficient for effective written communication. Many is the report I have seen which rambles on unstructured, verbose, and unedited. How many reports do you read which have a succinct summary, a brief introduction, a tightly written main report, and clear, well presented, well substantiated conclusions and recommendations?

The Superboss doesn't go into writing unless it is absolutely necessary, but sometimes it is necessary. He doesn't produce a stream of off-the-cuff memos as a lazy substitute for face-to-face communication, but he does produce the occasional written report to his boss, his colleagues, and his subordinates. It will be well researched, well presented, and well written.

In his written report the Superboss will differentiate between facts and opinions, between conclusions and recommendations, between assumptions and assertions.

The skill of writing is an essential one for management, but it is a neglected skill.

ACTION TODAY

Examine your last three written reports and severely criticize them. Analyze each report and mark it out of 20 as follows:

Was there a clear summary?	Yes, less than 1/2 page	(2 marks)
	Yes, more than 1/2 page	(4 marks)
Was there an introduction?	Yes, less than 1 page	(2 marks)
	Yes, more than 1 page	4 marks

ou edit it before as sent out?	Yes, and more than $1/3$rd was rewritten	(2 marks)
	Yes, but little was changed	4 marks
Were there clear conclusions?	Yes, less than 1 page	(2 marks)
	Yes, more than 1 page	4 marks
Were there clear recommendations?	Yes, less than $1/2$ page	2 marks
	Yes, more than $1/2$ page	(1 mark)
Overall, was the report written in a clear, succinct, easy-to-read style?	Yes, I received compliments about the report	2 marks
	Yes, but I could have polished it a little more	(1 mark)

TOTAL FOR THE PERFECT REPORT   20 marks

ZEROING IN — SELECT YOUR TARGET AND ZERO IN ON IT.

The Superboss has learned not to be distracted by activities, problems, and meetings that are not connected with his target objectives.

He zeroes in on the real target and keeps his sights there, suppressing any selfish interest to pursue peripheral activities. All his energies are concentrated on what he has to achieve and he zeroes in on any problems which might stop him. If the target is increasing production levels this month, or decreasing stock levels in the warehouse, or recruiting some hard-to-find systems programmers, or introducing a new quality-control system, then he'll zero in on these targets and achieve them.

By zeroing in he focuses his team's attention on what really has to be achieved. Lack of focus would dissipate their efforts.

ACTION TODAY

Zero in on the biggest problem facing you today, whether it be an employee relations, financial, or output problem. Critically review your appointment book with your secretary and eliminate all "flak" activity, redeploying the time to the problem you're zeroing in on.

Be careful not to eliminate time with your boss, colleagues, or your staff. Their help is essential if you are to achieve your target.

But you can resign from committees which don't interest you, and postpone liaison visits which will profit you little, and cancel meetings which have no relevance to your target objectives.

Having identified the problem, having created the time, zero in and solve the problem.

REMEMBER

The SUPERBOSS zeroes in on managing people successfully, for that's the only way to achieve results.

INDEX